GAIA'S
SACRED
CHAKRA

Order this book online at www.trafford.com
or email orders@trafford.com

Most Trafford titles are also available at major online book retailers.

Print information available on the last page.

ISBN: 978-1-4120-1275-1 (sc)

Cover: Terry Pamplin

Trafford rev. 10/03/2019

 www.trafford.com

North America & international
toll-free: 1 888 232 4444 (USA & Canada)
fax: 812 355 4082

GAIA'S SACRED CHAKRAS:
A PERSONAL EXPLORATION OF THE RELATION BETWEEN
CHAKRAS AND SACRED PLACES

by

Margaret Bertulli

A Thesis

Submitted in Partial Satisfaction of the Requirements

for the Degree of

Master of Liberal Arts in Creation Spirituality

in the

Graduate Division

of

Naropa University

March 2002

Approved: Marlene DeNardo, D. Min., Advisor

Approved: John Jerry-Anthony Parente, D. Min., Reader

For Elg, who,

in the final stages of her terminal illness,

prayed for me

as I wrote this thesis.

CONTENTS

ILLUSTRATIONS

Illustration Credits

Figure
1.1   http://www.crystalinks.com/gaia.html
1.2   Earth Chakras, by M. Bertulli, 2001, 11" x 14" (image size), watercolour
2.1   http://www.arcus.org/alias
2.2   Arctic, by M. Bertulli, 2001, 11" x 14" (image size), watercolour
2.3 - 2.5 M. Bertulli
3.1   http://www.chalicewell.org.uk/where_are_we.html
3.2   http://www.chalicewell.org.uk/flow-forms.html
3.3 - 3.5 M. Bertulli
4.1   http://www.earthwisdom.com/arizonainfo.html

TABLES

MEDITATIONS

INTRODUCTION

Beginning
Fresh, innovative
Believing, begetting, birthing
The cycle of all possibility
End

As a professional archaeologist with an interest in photography, I have travelled frequently and extensively to many ancient sites and sacred places. It is only within the last several years that I have come to accept and understand the sacredness of certain places. In earlier years, my focus was primarily upon capturing photographic images of ancient buildings, monuments and nature, as attested to by the thousands of slides I have accumulated. I saw these beauteous wonders as objects, not as expressions of a rich and ancient symbolism with contemporary meaning. My experience and vision were shaped not only by my limited understanding of spirituality, but also by my repudiation of the subjective approach to comprehend new and, dare I now say, mystical experiences.

My spirituality is emerging through these recognized encounters with the sacred as identified by the symbols and imagery of ancient cultures. Henderson, a Jungian scholar, (1979: 97) says, "As archaeologists dig deep into the past, it is not the events of historical time that we learn to treasure but the statues, designs, temples and languages that tell of old beliefs."

This thesis is a personal exploration of seven ancient sites I have visited, each of which I relate to one of the seven major chakras. These sites, as well as many others, are sacred heritage. In travelling to a sacred place, one discovers the site's spiritual power within its actual setting. Each site is related to a specific chakra on the basis of my personal experience there and the symbolism and concept associated with the chakra. Thus my interpretation may differ from yours, should you visit one of these sites and use the meditation. Be open to all encounters. I assume the reader's basic familiarity with the chakra system but also include two appendices which adumbrate each chakra's major attributes and concepts.

Each chapter begins with an original poem and ends with a guided meditation. Writing poetry, while not new for me, was fulfilling and encouraging. I particularly enjoyed composing the cinquains in this Introduction, Chapter IX and Figure 2.1. This is an elegant form of poetry, the first line of which is a single noun; the second line is two adjectives; the third is three gerunds; the fourth is a phrase, and the fifth is a repetition or synonym of the first noun. (Ronzani 2002) All descriptors refer to the original noun and complex ideas can be explored, simply and elegantly, in as few as a dozen words.

The meditations are intended to work with the energies of the sacred site and its associated chakra. They are practical as well as conceptual. In other words, they can be used on site where the powerful aspect of place may come into play in invoking a deeper, connective experience with the site and the chakra it represents. Or they may be used conceptually, thousands of miles away; in this case, the site descriptions and recounting of my experience may provide the impetus for others to incubate their own. The archaeological site descriptions and photographs are intended to provide enough information for the reader to envision herself at the actual site while doing the meditations.

<   In the first meditation, with an arctic animal guide, we travel along a line of *inukshuit,* navigation markers made of piled stones in the shape of a person, to discover the gifts the land has to offer for our survival and those gifts we hold

inside.

< At the second site of Chalice Well in England, we engage in a meditation of forgiveness by connecting with the flowing waters of the Well through the sacral chakra's element of water and its attribute of allowing energy to pass through and transform.

< In the third meditation, we stretch our personal boundaries, using the element of fire, related to the solar plexus chakra.

< The fourth meditation with the heart chakra takes us to one of my favourite places, Glastonbury Tor in England, where we use the heart to see and accept wisdom.

< At the fifth site of Silbury Hill at Avebury in England, associated with the throat chakra, we use a sound meditation to find a mantra, entrained to the heartbeat of the universe.

< The intention of the meditation at Gavrinis in Brittany is to use the third eye of the brow chakra to travel to the past and reconnect with a time when life and death were equally accepted and venerated in society.

< The meditation with the crown chakra uses the timelessness of the Great Pyramid of Giza to encapsulate the gifts of the first six chakras and to generate an understanding of one's interconnection with all in the Universe.

I loved working on this thesis because I was able to draw upon my acknowledged capabilities while developing new, unrealized ones. Each person is a mystic and artist in some way (Naropa 2001), and I have appreciated finding and developing my ways in this program. It was a fully creative process with new ideas and understandings continually popping into my consciousness. I have enjoyed the time and necessity of reading and writing about archaeological sites, drawing upon many years of experience in the field.

I also include three watercolour paintings, the first three I have ever done, as they appear to me to be connected to what I am trying to convey in this thesis—the organic relationship between the Earth and human bodies. The images of each site at the end of Chapters II to VIII are prints from my slide collections of the past 20 years and it feels good to share them. The photographic images, the poetry and watercolours are intended to convey how art, nature and human activity are all reflections of the divine. Even rummaging around the Internet for appropriate side illustrations was fun.

The journey continues.

Chapter I

**The Gaia-Human Relationship of
Sacred Place and Chakra**

> I enter the sacred space
> and the world splits . . .
> apart,
> immediately, irrevocably.
> I am at the centre,
> even as I approach it, and . . .
> I am the centre.
> Time and space conflate.
> Freed spirit dances.

That the Earth lives is ancient knowledge transmitted from a time in the distant past when humans existed in and celebrated nature. Moreover, the Earth, as an intelligent entity, is capable of a significant if circumscribed range of action (Graves 1988), particularly with regard to its own survival.

North American indigenous peoples have long understood this concept. Shaman Rolling Thunder says, "The earth is a living organism, the body of a higher individual who has a will and wants to be well, who is at times healthy or more healthy, physically and mentally." (In Pettis 1999: 69)

In the late eighteenth century, geologist James Hutton likened the Earth to a superorganism whose appropriate study lay in the realm of physiology. This insight, disregarded in the conservative and reductionist views of nineteenth-century science, was revived with the Gaia Hypothesis of biochemist James Lovelock (1988) who wrote a biography of the Earth. Rooting the study of the Earth in physiology and biography, disciplines which deal with living organisms and human beings, underscores the theory's profundity and authenticity. With the collaboration of microbioloogist Lynn Margulis, the hypothesis has advanced to the rank of theory. Focussing on wonder, communion and interdependence, the theory posits that the Earth is a planetary being whose self-regulation ensures its continued existence; whose substance fosters interactions between living beings, and between living beings and nonliving components (rocks, atmosphere, oceans); and whose totality, greater than the sum of its parts, acts to harmonize each component's participation in a way which benefits the whole. "If the real world we inhabit is self-regulating . . . , and if the climate and environment we enjoy and freely exploit is a consequence of an automatic, but not purposeful, goal seeking system, then Gaia is the largest manifestation of life." (Lovelock 1988: 39) The theory's principle is elegantly simple: Through co-evolution, life has transformed and been transformed by the biosphere. Organisms, which persist and burgeon, are those which assist in sustaining the biosphere in ways that are beneficial for all life. Further, the definitions of *living* and *nonliving* begin to converge when we see that "over vast time rock transforms into living creatures which then eventually transform back into rock" (Pollack 1997:227).

The theory is appropriately named: *Gaia* is the name ancient Greeks gave to Mother Earth, Oldest of Divinities (Walker 1983:332); their myths speak of existence as beginning with Gaia (Pollack 1997: 22); but they probably adopted this earth goddess, from the people of Attica into whose lands the Greeks relocated (Monaghan 2000:39).

This understanding of Gaia as a planetary being was crystallized in 1970 when luminous images of Earth arrived from the depths of space. "Viewed from the distance

of the moon, the astonishing thing about the earth, catching the breath, is that it is alive."
(Lewis in Swan 1990: 210)

Gaia's range of action–regulation of temperature, ocean salinity and atmospheric gas levels–demonstrates her continual self-transforming capabilities; her actions occur at a planetary level, where humans are one of the millions of species and where human survival pivots upon a right relationship with Gaia. Gaia has been here, a most ancient presence, for 4.5 billion years. She has complexified into beauty to the point where she is now able to see and know herself through the conscious self-awareness of humans. Human consciousness is necessary for Gaia to acknowledge herself.

In my opinion, the acceptance of the Gaia Theory leads to rich and fertile realms from which to launch studies in all disciplines and endeavours. It is meaningful on intuitive, experiential, scientific, spiritual, metaphysical, philosophical, artistic and ethical planes (Sahtouris 1999). Thus, the nexus of Earth body and human body encourages understanding and acceptance of the similarities and diversities of living and nonliving beings, empathy and reciprocity between humans and other beings, and deep awareness of our sedimentedness in the Earth. We meet Gaia in the land and the landscape is where we exist.

The human body recapitulates Gaia's body since both are composed of the same elements, particles and energies. "All the energy that would ever exist in the entire course of time erupted as a single quantum–a singular gift–existence." (Swimme and Berry 1994:17) Given this understanding, I believe it is possible to apply the concept of chakras to the Earth's body.

Sanskrit for wheel or disk, the *chakras* are a metaphysical complex of seven major vortices within the human body that manifest levels of consciousness, behaviour, colours, sounds, and vibrations, and are indicative of the progression of individual psycho-spiritual development as well as socio-cultural evolution. The seven major chakras–root, sacrum, solar plexus, heart, throat, brow and crown–are centres found along the spine of the human body where energies are received, assimilated and

transmitted. As physical and metaphorical centres, they constitute the "connecting channel between body and mind, spirit and matter, past and future, Heaven and Earth" (Judith 1990: 1)–in other words, a philosophical model of the Universe.

The earliest reference to chakras is in the Vedas, the sacred scriptures of hymns and rituals of Hinduism, dated to 2000 - 600 BCE. Here it is written that Vishnu, the male deity known as the protector of the Universe, descended to Earth, carrying in his four arms a chakra or conch, a lotus, a club or mace, and a conch shell. The later Upanishads (700 - 300 BCE) contain references to the chakras as meditational foci; 10th- and 16th-century yoga texts contribute to the spread of current appreciation of the chakra theory to the West through translation in the 1920s. (Judith 1990:9; Vishnu 2000)

Figure 1.1: Blue Woman Circle

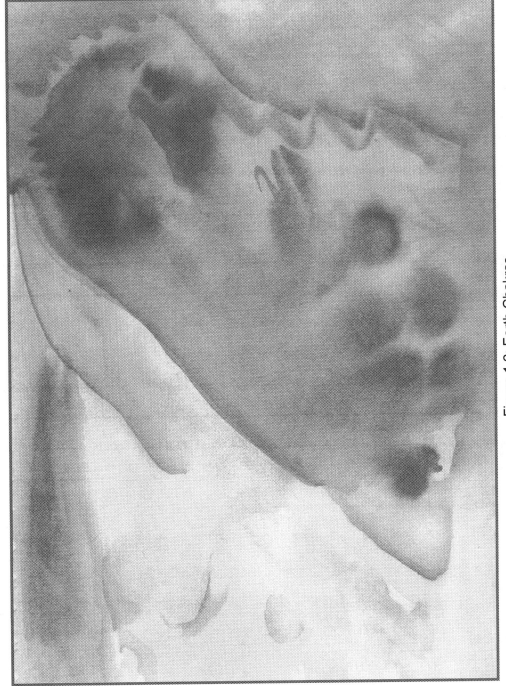

Figure 1.2: Earth Chakras

Sanskrit for wheel or disk, the *chakras* are a metaphysical complex of seven major vortices within the human body that manifest levels of consciousness, behaviour, colours, sounds, and vibrations, and are indicative of the progression of individual psycho-spiritual development as well as socio-cultural evolution. The seven major chakras–root, sacrum, solar plexus, heart, throat, brow and crown–are centres found along the spine of the human body where energies are received, assimilated and transmitted. As physical and metaphorical centres, they constitute the "connecting channel between body and mind, spirit and matter, past and future, Heaven and Earth" (Judith 1990: 1)–in other words, a philosophical model of the Universe.

The earliest reference to chakras is in the Vedas, the sacred scriptures of hymns and rituals of Hinduism, dated to 2000 - 600 BCE. Here it is written that Vishnu, the male deity known as the protector of the Universe, descended to Earth, carrying in his four arms a chakra or conch, a lotus, a club or mace, and a conch shell. The later Upanishads (700 - 300 BCE) contain references to the chakras as meditational foci; 10[th-] and 16th-century yoga texts contribute to the spread of current appreciation of the chakra theory to the West through translation in the 1920s. (Judith 1990:9; Vishnu 2000)

Each chakra is related to a specific energy centre in the body as a gateway to expanding physical, emotional and spiritual connections. Their role is to act as a specific centre for transforming energies. It is also well to remember that "the chakras are in constant interplay and can only be separated intellectually" (Judith 1990: 45); each is a synthesis of the consciousness of upper and lower levels.

The characteristics of the seven major chakras are adumbrated in Table 1.1. Appendix A lists characteristics specific to each chakra. Appendix B shows how the assemblage of chakra knowledge has been employed as an organizing construct by various authors to discuss healing and illness (Myss 1996, Northrup 1994, Schultz 1998); mythic imagery (Campbell 1974); sin and blessings (Fox 1999); consciousness (Judith 1990); and logical levels of neuro-linguistic programming (LeBrun 1997).

Table 1.1: Key Concepts of the Seven Major Chakras

1	Root (Muladhara)	groundedness, survival, physical security, connection to body and physicality
2	Sacral (Svadhisthana)	emotions, sexuality, movement,
3	Solar plexus (Manipura)	self-definition, independence,
4	Heart (Anahata)	love, compassion, connection, integration of opposites
5	Throat (Visshudha)	communication, creativity, expression
6	Brow (Ajna)	physical and intuitive perception, communication with the divine
7	Crown (Sahasrara)	spiritual awareness, ecstasy, connection with the divine

References: http://www.healinghappens.com/chakras.htm; http://www.sacredcentres.com

As the human body is the place where the soul manifests itself (O'Donohue 1998), sacred places are amongst those where Gaia shows herself and her energies. I believe sacred places exist on the Earth as chakras exist in the human body. The conjunction of energies at sacred places can be analysed as Gaia's chakras for sacred places stimulate each of the seven levels of consciousness represented by the chakras in individual as well as universal ways. Such places, often called *earth chakras*, have long been acknowledged by local populations as places where the invisible connects

with the visible, and spirit with matter (Coon 2001) From base to crown, some of the
corresponding Cardinal Earth Chakras are:

<   Mount Shasta, California, USA; Mount Sinai, Egypt
<   Lake Titicaca, Peru; an unspecified place in Brazil near the Amazon River
<   Uluru-Katatjuta (Ayers Rock), Australia; Kilimanjaro, Tanzania
<   Glastonbury, England; Haleakala, Hawaii, USA
<   Great Pyramid of Cheops, Egypt; Mount of Olives, Israel; Mount Shasta, California, USA
<   Kuh-e-Malek Siah, Iran; Himalaya Mountains
<   Mount Kailes, Tibet; Fujiyama, Japan. (Vortexes 2001; Royal 1995)

The planetary distribution of sacred places, the millennia throughout which
humans have created and venerated them, and the tremendous effort and social
organization required to construct them attest to the universal significance of their
existence. Sacred places move and quicken the soul, bringing one to a higher
consciousness. The psychical and physical grounding they provide through a sense of
place elicits awe and wonder. The presence and flow of earth energies at sacred places
heightens human sensibilities and assists in achieving intensified spiritual growth by
stimulating human chakras.

Whether certain places have an inherent sacredness or whether people sacralize
them is a matter of perspective; the accumulation of sacred energy at a site is
established by tradition and by human-Gaian interaction. "The singular magic of a place
is evident from what happens there, from what befalls oneself or others when in its
vicinity. To tell of such events is implicitly to tell of the particular power of that site, and
indeed to participate in its expressive potency." (Abrams 1997: 182) Mystical

experiences, which open one to the awe and wonder of the Universe and establish,

even fleetingly, a psychic connection between disparate beings and entities, often occur

in these special places. I, too, find that I am more receptive to such experiences at

places where sacred heritage exists.

What attributes identify sacred places? The following compilation is from Peck

(1995:71), Brockman (1998: vii), Devereux (2000: 150; 2001), Osmen (1990) and

Harpur (1994: 7-9).

- < Natural beauty
- < Ancient and historical human construction
- < Association with an historical event, prophet, saint, miracle, apparition, healing, or religious ritual
- < Ancestral or mythical dwellings of gods and goddesses; legendary places
- < Evil or horrific events of great consequence
- < Manifestation of earth energies or the numinous influences of nature
- < Aesthetic, spiritual and cultural energies
- < Burial sites
- < Sources of sacred materials
- < Locales for dream divination and for seeking visions
- < Transformative places where one may travel to the spirit world
- < Numinosity or the presence of good and bad elements, and liminality
- < Mystery and alchemy
- < Proximity to fault lines or places of tectonic strain, magnetic and gravitational aberration, or variable electromagnetic fields
- < A human presence to behold. "Landscape was here on its own. It is the most ancient presence in the world, though it needs a human presence to acknowledge it." (O'Donohue 1998: 37)

I describe sacred places to which I have travelled and relate each to one of the

seven major chakras, beginning with the root chakra and ending with the crown. This

sequence is usually followed because working with the chakras is like climbing a ladder.

By opening and incorporating the energy of each chakra in ascending order, one may

achieve enlightenment or a transcendent consciousness.

TABLE 1.2: ASSOCIATIONS BETWEEN EACH SITE AND CHAKRA

Muladhara: Root chakra
John Richardson Bay,
Ellesmere Island,
and
King William Island,
Arctic Canada

The first chakra's characteristic of survival is linked to the John Richardson Bay in the High Canadian Arctic where human living conditions are marginal and where ancient hunters used ingenuity and skill to survive on the land. King William Island in the Mid Canadian Arctic shows how the failure of a mid-nineteenth century British expedition to listen to land's wisdom ended in starvation, cannibalism and death for 129 men. Earth is the element of the base chakra; in the Earth is survival rooted.

Svadisthana: Sacral chakra
Chalice Well,
Glastonbury, England

Water is the element that integrates the sacral chakra and Chalice Well. With the feminine aspect of water, we seek absolution and freedom to move and expand, to grow consciously. This is what the contemplative gardens and Chalice Well offer.

Manipura: Solar plexus chakra
Bell Rock, Sedona, USA

The energy of this chakra calls us to action in large and small ways; it calls us to know ourselves and bring this knowledge into the world with will and intention. Using the energy of this chakra, I was able to accomplish what for me was a significant feat.

Anahata: Heart chakra
Glastonbury Tor, England

Love, compassion, and wholeness fuel this chakra whose element is air. Entering Glastonbury is like entering another reality where the air itself is dense with meaning and potential. Here one can easily see the coexistence of past and present as temporal linearity fades and the richest legends from the deep past remain alive.

Visshudha: Throat chakra
Avebury, England

This chakra is also called the gateway to consciousness; it subsumes communication, truth-telling and interconnection, necessary components in ceremony and ritual. Here, I have associated the Avebury Complex, a large ceremonial centre on the Wiltshire Downs and one of the most important spiritual foci of Neolithic Britain.

Ajna: Brow chakra
Gavrinis, France

This chakra is related to clairvoyance, "a willed process of visualization" (Judith 1990:338) of which we are all capable. It is also related to imagination and intuition. At Gavrinis, these qualities became operative in a past-life regression I underwent.

Sahasrara: Crown chakra
Great Pyramid of Khufu,
El Giza, Egypt

The energy of this chakra relates to knowing, understanding and communicating the interconnection of all in creation. Almost five thousand years ago, an advanced civilization created enduring monuments symbolizing its connection with the Universe. "It is not trite for the African to say 'everything is everything'." (Asante 2000: 2)

Chapter II

The Base Chakra and the Canadian Arctic

To others, this land is desolate and harsh,
distant, vast,
featureless in winter whiteness
where unremitting longing prevails.
To me, this is land of eternal vista,
tracking from me to the North Pole
with no one in between.
At my feet, the tundra lives with tiny flowers.
The celestial dome, unobstructed by human artifact,
white contrail in bluest sky, cradles me.
My kin, ancient hunters, walked here before me,
surviving with the bounty of Nuna, the Land.

Far from the populated stretch of temperate zone, the Canadian Arctic extends across 35 degrees of latitude and 80 degrees of longitude. Within this largely unpeopled vastness of 1.5 million square kilometres exist unique, vibrant, and intricate networks of natural and cultural phenomena. Although the words *harsh* and *desolate* are often applied to this ecozone, its rich diversity, challenging conditions and extreme isolation manifest ingenious adaptations and breathtaking spectacles. All, from the unobstructed skies with kaleidoscopic displays of northern lights to the diminutive vegetation underfoot, is a marvel of adaptation and survival.

I chose an ancient hunting site on John Richardson Bay, Ellesmere Island, as an example of interdependent living for survival, and King William Island, as an example of independence leading to tragedy, to represent aspects of the root chakra. Both of these are places of natural beauty; the former is a site of past human existence at the beginning of the last millennium, and the latter is a site of human tragedy in the mid-nineteenth century. The Inuit and their predecessors have lived in the Canadian Arctic for more than four thousand years. Using the resources of the land–skins, snow, stone and bone—and their considerable ingenuity, they have survived in a marginal and difficult environment, complicated by winter darkness. This was possible, in part, through increasing specialization in marine mammal hunting as well as the recognition of interdependence in the form of kinship with humans and animals.

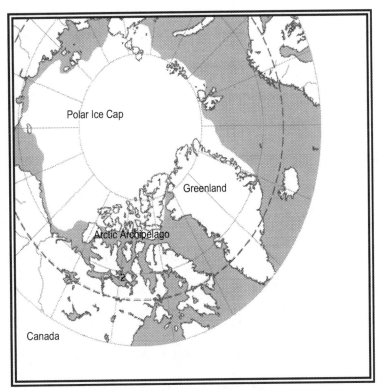

Figure 2.1: Location of John Richardson Bay (1) and King
William Island (2), Canadian Arctic.

Named after the nineteenth-century British surgeon-naturalist and explorer, John Richardson Bay extends into the northeastern coast of Ellesmere Island, ten degrees of latitude from the North Geographic Pole. Seas are frozen for about ten months of the year, and the barren land rises in stepped gravel beaches to the encircling highlands. As soon as the helicopter disgorged me, my colleague and our gear, and the thwacking of its rotors subsided into the distance, I was overcome by the familiar, anticipated sensation of being alone at the top of the world, both literally and figuratively. In pervasive silence, we gazed across the expansive gravel beaches broken only by the patterns of stones put in place centuries ago by people building shelters and cooking places, and clumps of vegetation telling of underlying archaeological deposits. The day was cool, grey and still with the overcast skies contriving the rarified effect of mirroring the mountains opposite in the leaden waters of the bay.

The root chakra is concerned with physical survival, grounding, earth, security, one's connection to the physical world and one's place within the larger group or community, which includes living and nonliving beings. It harkens to a time when life was precarious and depended on the efficacy of this chakra. "In early times, concern for survival was the primary focus of consciousness— and with it we built a foundation, a culture" (Judith 1990:75), through explicit relation with the arctic seasons, animals, land and sea. The base chakra also represents the Earth; ultimately, all survival, and particularly the survival of human hunting cultures, depends upon the Earth. "The solid matter of our bodies is kept alive by the solid matter from the Earth, in the form of food, clothing and shelter." (Judith 1990: 78) This balance is not disrupted on a large scale by ancient hunters.

On the northernmost reaches of Ellesmere Island, 1000 years ago, Arctic hunters lived in structures composed of stone, turf and skins. Called the *Late Dorset* people by archaeologists, they survived by depending upon land mammals such as the polar bear and sea mammals such as beluga, narwhal, seals and walrus for the means of their entire subsistence and material culture; in other words, with only the immediate resources of the land and sea available to them and with the use of prehistoric stone and bone technology, the Dorset fashioned an enduring existence with physical and spiritual comforts. They developed specialized artifacts for living on the sea ice and hunting marine mammals: intricate bone harpoons attached to shafts of bone or driftwood, large bone knives for cutting blocks of snow to construct snow houses, snow-creepers or crampons for walking on ice; soapstone lamps for burning sea mammal fat for heat and light Depending upon the bounty of the land, as well as a prodigious knowledge of tool-making, animal lore, weather, and hunting skills, the Dorset people evinced a deliberate will to encounter both physical danger and spiritual challenge. Groundedness, a characteristic of the root chakra, is an essential aspect of a hunting culture through the acknowledgement of one's interdependence with the Earth and its other creatures. Further, groundedness allows the individual hunter to intuit, assimilate and then act upon those variables that interact to conclude in a successful hunt, which is fraught with danger particularly when in pursuit of large prey. This characteristic enables the hunter to focus on the requirements of the present moment. The root chakra is also related to a diet high in meats and proteins, which remain in the digestive tract longer than other foods and contribute to one's groundedness. Lacking in the vegetal resources of southern regions, ancient arctic peoples relied upon a diet of uncooked meat and fat, rich in protein and vitamins.

In the latter stages of the Dorset period, their lifeways altered significantly. Archaeologists speculate that a warming climate caused altered sea ice conditions with concomitant changes in the distribution of sea mammals upon which the Dorset people depended. Traditional hunting patterns were no longer reliable, there is evidence of trade, movement and migration and an artistic fluorescence of intricate bone and ivory carvings.

The Dorset peoples' legacy lies in these beautiful, miniature figures; they attest not only to consummate artistic skill but also to a belief in a spiritual realm based on shamanism, an ideology which acknowledges that animals as well as humans have .

Figure 2.1: Arctic Watercolour and Cinquain
Arctic / Icy, singular / Freezing, thawing, beautifying / Bringing me to my soul / North

souls. It is not surprising that most likenesses depicted in Dorset art are animals, since human sustenance necessitates the appropriation of animal life. Seeing the spiritual aspect of material existence is also a characteristic of the root chakra. (Judith 1990: 80)

We do not know what happened to the Dorset people. The threat of starvation, disease, and the invasion of the Thule Inuit, technologically superior newcomers from the West, may have contributed to their assimilation and disappearance from the archaeological record. Inuit legends speak of a people called the *Tunit* who were forced from the arctic regions by their Thule successors, and it is widely understood that the people whom archaeologists call "Dorset" are the *Tunit* of legend. (McGhee 2001)

The British Royal Navy's Expedition of 1845 to the Canadian Arctic was also an allegory of survival in relation to the root chakra. Unfortunately, all expeditioners perished. One interpretation is that the extreme independence with which the Royal Navy approached this task, discounting the accumulated wisdom of the people who had occupied this land for centuries, was a contributing factor. This is the story.

Graves of three members of the Franklin expedition who died on Beechey Island.

In July 1845, Sir John Franklin and his crew of 129 men, aboard two proven vessels, entered the waters of the Canadian High Arctic in search of the Northwest Passage. Ironically, Franklin's party was the largest and best equipped sent by the British Admiralty to the Arctic Archipelago in quest of a navigable northern route to the Far East. After entering the Archipelago, they were never again seen by Europeans. From Inuit oral knowledge and historical and archaeological reconnaissance, we are able to piece together the clues which partially reveal the expedition's fate.

Franklin's ships, *H.M.S. Erebus* and *H.M.S. Terror*, were beset by ice to the north of King William Island, in September 1846 and remained so over the next summer and winter. A note left in a cairn on the island's northwest coast conveyed the information that Franklin had died in June 1847 and that the 105 remaining crew members, led by the second-in-command, would begin a trek south along the western coast of King William Island toward sanctuary. After leaving the icebound ships in April 1848, all perished. Neither records of the expedition nor the ships themselves have ever been found. Inuit oral knowledge contributes that the men resorted to cannibalism to extend their lives, and that many dropped and died as they trekked along the low-lying, featureless terrain. Search voyages found expeditioners' remains lying in face-down postures, unburied on the ground surface, and the physical evidence of butchering marks on the skeletal remains corroborate the allegation of cannibalism (Keenleyside, Bertulli and Fricke 1997). The news, once returned to England, that Franklin's men had resorted to cannibalism so affronted Britons' sensitivities that controversy raged. (Bertulli ND) Yet, in extreme circumstances, cannibalism is a logical reaction, related to the survival message of the root chakra.

Incorporating the lesson of this chakra means to accept individual wholeness as well as one's role and place in the greater whole. (Judith 1990: 95) The British explorers' illusions of separateness from the land and the accumulated knowledge of the people who had lived on it successfully for generations led to their demise.

Meditation for a Journey from the Base Chakra to the Arctic:

Attunement with the Earth

Prepare yourself for a journey of healing, self-knowledge and interdependence. Winter is the season of the Arctic and the base chakra. Take with you those

things you need for survival–perhaps a cloak lined with hollow-haired caribou skin for warmth and a pair of bone snow goggles carved with narrow slits to prevent blindness from the intense reflection of sun on snow. Recall your intimate knowledge of the geography of the landscape, both inner and outer. Remember the ways of the animals, your guides. Attach a pair of spiked snow-creepers to your boots to give you purchase on the wind-polished snow and ice. Grasping your sewing kit and harpoon, you prepare to see the wonders of the Arctic. Take all that you need, but remember that you must carry and safeguard all that you take.

Step from your root chakra into the limitless land. At first, you can discern no boundaries, no demarcations. Your eyes stretch to the horizons–ten kilometres or ten hundred–you have no way of knowing how far because there are no vertical objects, no buildings or trees, to define distance or depth. The sun is visible through light cloud and it reflects blindingly on the snowy landscape. You are alone in the vastness, where the very silence is a presence, a welcome companion.

You don your snow goggles and, gradually, your eyes adjust to the brightness. You see that you are accompanied by a land mammal, perhaps a polar bear, arctic fox or wolf, and a bird, perhaps a tern or a raven. Thank them for their presence and ask them what knowledge each has to share with you. They accompany you on this journey.

Along the top of the nearby ridge, you see a shape. It looks like a person but it is an inukshuk, a stone form made to resemble a person. For hundreds of years, your predecessors have built these inukshuit as navigational aids or caribou drive lanes or as an expression of grief at the place where a loved one died.

What is this inukshuk telling you?

Do you hear her voice in the wind? Listen for a few moments.

Your eyes wander along the ridge and you see another inukshuk, then another and another–a line of them stretching toward the horizon. Where are they leading? To safety and security, to tests of physical endurance? Will you follow? The cold creeps through your bones. You had not noticed it, but now you pull your cloak snugly around your shoulders as you step forward with your guides, your snow-creepers biting into the hardened snow. You are resolved. Reaching the first inukshuk, you scan the surrounding terrain, and then looking at your feet, you see that the land has a gift for you. You pick it up and hold it in your hand, savouring its texture and shape. What knowledge does it hold for you and what information do your guides give you about this gift? Folding it into your voluminous cloak, you trek to the next inukshuk. Here, too, the land has a gift. You accept it, as you understand its insight and intent. With your animal guides, you follow the line of inukshuit to the horizon; at each stone-being there is a gift, which you may accept or reject. You acknowledge each, giving thanks to the provider. You travel from inukshuk to inukshuk in this way until you gain the horizon where sitting, *you spread your gifts on your cloak. Examining each of them in turn, you reflect on your strengths and abilities, your opportunities and your challenges. What do these symbols signify for you?*

The short day ends while you are engaged in this reverie. The greenish-yellow aurora borealis swirls and whooshes 1000 kilometres above your head. From groundedness, you open to wonder and delight. Gathering your gifts, thanking your guides and the Universe which has provided all the gifts of creation, you return to your root chakra. What energy do you feel here?

As you emerge from this meditation, both you and your world are different.

Figure 2.3: Arctic poppies and icebergs in August, Slidre Fiord, Ellesmere Island,
Canadian High Arctic.

Figure 2.4: Reflections, John Richardson Bay, Ellesmere Island

Figure 2.5: Skeletal remains of members of the British Royal Navy's
Expedition in 1845 to the Canadian Arctic. These remains lay exposed until recovered
by an archaeological expedition in 1993 (Keenleyside, Bertulli and Fricke 1997).

Chapter III

The Sacral Chakra and the Waters of Chalice Well, Glastonbury, England

Soul-soothing stillness,
Stifled sobbing.
Release and rebirth.
The Well works its magic.
The Well's magic works.

As energies flow from the root to the sacral chakra, unity becomes dual, the solid (earth) becomes a liquid (water), and stillness becomes movement. With this change are introduced complexity and awareness of the other, as symbolized by the *yin-yang*, the feminine and the masculine, each of which balances and encloses the other (Judith 1990: 114-5), as complementarities rather than dualities. To dance the embodiment of paradox, to avoid extremes and maintain centre is the overture of the sacral chakra; this is accomplished by espousing one's masculine and feminine energies.

In complement to the root chakra, which is correlated with *yang* or masculine energy, *Svadhisthana*, the sacral chakra, is primarily associated with *yin* or feminine qualities of receptivity and nurturance. It is also related to the moon, to water and to sexuality. The sacral chakra calls for us to admit our desires. Acknowledging, rather than denying one's desires, allows one to effect movement, which leads to change, upon which consciousness thrives. "Like the moon's pull on the tides, our desires and passions can move great oceans of energy." (Judith 1990: 121)

Chalice Well in Glastonbury, England represents the second energy centre, and water is the central symbol which relates sacred site to sacral chakra.

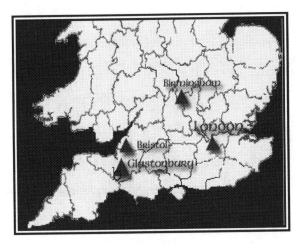

Figure 3.1: Location of Glastonbury in
Southwestern England

Located on the flank of Glastonbury Tor (hill) at the town's edge, the Well and

Gardens possess sweeping views of the countryside as well as private spaces. A sense

of timelessness and mythic reality pervade the contemplative gardens, where the

sounds of traffic are muffled. The well and fountains are surrounded by medieval

stonework. One of the oldest holy wells in England, Chalice Well has been used since

prehistoric times and certainly for the last 2000 years. The well shaft is thought to date

to the thirteenth century BCE. (Chalice Well Gardens: ND)

From subterranean caverns rushes the Blood Spring of Chalice Well. Flowing at

a rate of 25,000 gallons each day without diminishment (Mann 1993: 54), the high iron

content of the water, said to be the menstrual blood of the goddess, stains the conduits

and fountains through which it flows a rusty red colour.

The wrought iron design of the wellhead cover is most

striking. It is the ancient symbol of the *vesica piscis* (vessel of

fish), which, like *yin-yang,* represents the male and female in

perfect balance. It consists of two interlocking circles whose

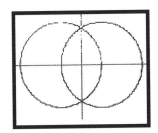

pointed-oval conjunction denotes the female yoni, "the gate of earthly existence and spiritual knowledge" (Howard-Gordon 1982: 21). Running longitudinally through the interlocking circles is a line or sword, male symbol of force and a second-chakra attribute. Circling these symbols are curvilinear flowering vines, evident in the landscape today. For me, the *vesica* is a symbol of the intrinsic unity of the human species without gender distinction, and by extension, our interconnectedness with all in the Universe.

From the wellhead, water flows through the Gardens arising at the Lion's Head Fountain, then King Arthur's Court where it was once deep enough to bathe in, and finally pours through the Sevenfold Metamorphic Cascade. Here the water descends through a series of seven *flowforms* or shapes that denote the birth canal and labia onto a phallic protuberance in the *vesica*-shaped pool.

Again, the relationship to the sexual energy of the sacral chakra is apparent. In harmony with the sacral chakra, the waters of the Cascade represent the waters of menstruation or birth.

Each flowform is a vessel with a narrow entrance and exit, and a basin-like cavity through which the water's flow is regulated. The egress of each flowform is proportioned to create enough resistance for the outpouring waters to swirl in the alternating cavities, from right to left, in the pattern of a figure eight. Vortices of water form in each lobe.

Figure 3.2: Flowforms of the Metamorphic Cascade

Accustomed to its ubiquity, we regard water as a familiar substance rather than a magical one. Its magic lies in transporting and transforming energy in harmonic movement, in sustaining life processes.

Only fifty metres from Chalice Well and the outlet of the Red Spring, emerges the White Spring from an artesian source under nearby Glastonbury Tor. Its composition is calciferous rather than chalybeate, and its flow varies from 5,000 to 70,000 gallons a day (Mann 1993:55). Its waters are said to be the *milk of the goddess* (Stewart: personal communication) or the *waters of ovulation* (Griffyn 2000: 144). For centuries, the healing properties of both wells have been recognized.

I wear a pewter *vesica piscis* pendant almost constantly, and am pleasantly surprised by people who recognize it and connect with me through it. Others remark on the beauty of the design and ask me what it means. Finding Chalice Well at Glastonbury was a powerful experience. Long before I decided to undertake this journey, I found a drawing of the *vesica piscis* in Jean Shinoda Bolen's book, *Crossing to Avalon,* and was highly attracted to it. I used the design in artistic projects, making several and giving them to friends. I later learned that recopying such designs is a spiritual practice. On arrival at the retreat house at Chalice Well, I saw a picture of the same *vesica piscis* that I had been copying for several months. The Guardian of the Well explained that this was the design at the wellhead and I felt a huge sense of wonder to have been lead to this very place.

Huge yew trees, masculine symbols of immortality through death and resurrection and often planted in sacred Celtic groves (Walker 1988: 476), dominate the meditative gardens of Chalice Well. The remains of 2500-year-old yew trees have been recovered in the gardens. The yew's association with blood is clear.

> Yew bark is red and if pierced will bleed copious amounts
> of red sap. The tree also has red berries which can be

poisonous. The wood was traditionally used for making
coffins as well as dagger handles and long bows—weapons
for drawing blood. (Mann 1993: 55)

Chalice Well is a powerful spiritual place for me, a cathartic one, where the air and water are presences. In a guided meditation on forgiveness at the wellhead, I was lead to begin the path to forgiveness for real and imagined wrongs that I, as a woman, had suffered in patriarchal society. The symbol for this forgiveness came in the form of my own father and I realized that forgiving the father was a metaphorical way of accepting and empowering my masculine energies.

A few months after this initial visit, I was again drawn to Glastonbury from northern Canada. As I returned to Chalice Well, I bid farewell to my travelling companion, wheeled my luggage through the gate, and dashed to the wellhead with great relief. Dusk had descended. In the unilluminated blackness peculiar to English small towns, I stood, held by the dense air, inhaling and absorbing the energies of the Blood Spring from the open wellhead, as sobs rose from my depths. I shed the accumulated hurts and pangs of years, and I stayed until my sobs quieted.

Meditation with the Flowing Waters of Chalice Well and the Sacral Chakra

You stand on Chilkwell Street in Glastonbury, at the entrance to Chalice Well and its gardens. Cars flash by on the left side of the street; people in the neighbouring brick houses are stirring, and the local pub is closed at this hour of the early morning. A shepherd ventures onto the roadway, leading a flock of sheep to pasturage on the flanks of a nearby conical hill. Your North American sensibilities see this as an incongruous mix of the rural and urban, and you smile in secret excitement.

All is at it should be, here, where the veil between the worlds is diaphanous, and motorists wait patiently while sheep cross the road.

The air tingles in your nostrils as you stride along the flagstone path to the entrance of the Well and its Gardens. Inlaid in the path is the beguiling design of the vesica piscis; you linger in admiration and feel it resonate in your sacral chakra.

The Guardian of the Well smiles at you as you pass by her in silent reverie.

You arrive at the wellhead and listen to the rushing water.

Stimulate your sacral chakra with alternate nostril breathing. Blocking your right nostril with your right thumb, slowly and deeply inhale through your left one. Block your left nostril with your forefinger and exhale through your right nostril. Inhale through your right nostril, block it with your thumb, and exhale through your left nostril. This is one *complete round; repeat it at least ten times.*

You feel balanced and have a profound sense of well-being.

This chakra summons you to remain centred, to dance with paradox. The paradox is

that you acknowledge and love equally both the masculine

and feminine aspects of your psyche.

Slowly, your preoccupations with the material world dissipate, and from the centre of

your abdomen, your body dissolves into molecules of oxygen and hydrogen; you dive

into the flowing, ancient waters of Chalice Well.

This is an opportunity to move, to change, to yield to paradox.

You flow in luminescent caverns under the ancient hills, reduced to elements. You may

want to shed outmoded beliefs and practices which no longer serve. Perhaps you want

to forgive unconditionally someone who has transgressed against you. Think of a

behaviour pattern you want to change or someone whom it is now time to forgive. Form

a clear image or intent in your mind. You are joined to this pattern or this person by

cords of gold. The cords are beautiful but they hold you; you are now ready to leave

behind this shadow. Gently, and with due consideration, sever the cords with a sword.

As you do so, the cords disappear and you float buoyantly in the waters, born aloft and

cradled by waves. The sacral chakra also calls us to acknowledge our desires and

emotions; in this way, we move and develop. What is your present desire?

Slowly return your consciousness to the wellhead. There you stand in the sanctuary

formed by the enveloping yew trees and ancient walls. You feel freed. Your nostrils

tingle from breathing the heavily ionized air. You remember your chakra's desire.

Figure 3.3: Chalice Well Gardens with yew trees.

Figure 3.4: The Chalice Well and the *vesica piscis*

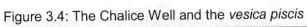

Figure 3.5: The Sevenfold Metamorphic Cascade
at Chalice Well Gardens

Chapter IV

The Solar Plexus Chakra and Bell Rock, Sedona, USA

My will.
Cosmic will.
If I will to do another's will,
whose will am I following?
Will, desire, and action in alignment.
Transformation.

Manipura, the solar plexus chakra, combines the physicality of the base chakra with the movement of the sacral chakra to yield combustive energies of power and will. Its element is fire, which signifies action and the assumption of responsibility in both inner and outer worlds. It is in *Manipura* where the earth of the root chakra and the water of the sacral chakra are alloyed into the mode of transformation. Fire betokens exertion and force; with its integration, we are able to control and forge our desires, to take conscious, intentional action, presupposed by choice and will. "Will is the . . . combination of mind and action, the overcoming of inertia, and the essential spark that ignites the flames of our power." (Judith 1990: 169)

The undertaking of the solar plexus chakra, then, is to prevail over inaction through the appropriate application of will. In physical terms, will provides the impetus which creates heat (power) to galvanize our movement into new forms of consciousness.

This exploration with the solar plexus chakra took me finally to Bell Rock, Sedona, Arizona, USA. For weeks, I meditated and mulled over which sacred site to relate to this chakra. I came up with

several ideas, but all lacked the unequivocal *Aha!* I sought. It was through a meditation

on Uluru-Katatjuta (Ayers Rock), Australia, the Cardinal Third Earth Chakra, that I

realized the conjunction of *Manipura* and Bell Rock in my

journey with the chakras.

Figure 4.1: Location of Sedona, Arizona, USA

Sedona's stark beauty of unique red-rock formations

in a desert landscape immediately attracted my

archaeologist's eye. I found the mesas and pinnacles of

hematitic rocks, sculpted throughout eons of geologic time,

fascinating and powerful, particularly from an aerial

panorama. Ten thousand years ago, Native Americans appreciated this natural

grandeur. The Sinagua, cliff-dwelling horticulturalists, lived and practised horticulture in

the area in the early part of the last millennium; their

pictographs are yet visible at the nearby ruins of Honanki

and Palatki. Legends tell of an immense flood from which a

young girl was saved by being secured in a log. Her

grandson later killed giant monsters that lived in the area;

their physical remnants are said to be the rock formations of

Sedona, and it is their blood which has made the rocks red.

Depending upon your perspective, Sedona is decried or epitomized as the centre

of New Age spirituality and mysticism. It claims several vortices, emanations of electric,

magnetic or electromagnetic energy from within the Earth said to affect human

consciousness and physiology. "Sedona has good vibes." (Jaffe 1996:1) The vortices

are considered to be intersections of telluric lines where auras and sounds have been observed.

Bell Rock, rising more than 60 metres in height, is said to have electric energy which equates to a strong masculine or active energy; it resonates with an individual's energy in idiosyncratic ways, generally by strengthening one's masculine energy. Adherents of this theory point to the twisted juniper trees growing out of cracks in the rock as evidence of the vortex's power. (Vortex Energy ND)

My companions and I determined to climb Bell Rock. The first part of the climb is fairly easy walking but the last, bell-shaped face is steep and difficult for those without experience. In the past, climbers have plummeted to their death in the attempt to reach the summit.

I climbed Bell Rock! (I end the previous sentence with an exclamation mark, lest the import of this achievement is lost on the reader.) I have a moderate fear of heights and have generally avoided them. Unfortunately, I discovered the strength of this fear in the Guatemalan jungle, at the top of the Temple of the Masks on the ancient Mayan site of Tikal. It is a steep, stepped pyramid, 40 metres high; realizing that a misstep would have undesirable, if not fatal, results I was paralysed to descend until assistance arrived.

The danger I inherently sense in high places causes my root and sacral chakras to vibrate most unpleasantly. I used this knowledge to climb Bell Rock. I paid attention to these sensations and pushed myself to the point where they verged on the unpleasant but were manageable. By periodically stopping to assess my progress, I was able to stretch the boundaries of my comfort and continue the climb. Eventually my companions and I arrived at a small plateau within sight of the summit; only two of us proceeded. At this point, we met a woman named Diana who was enjoying the dramatic view from a decidedly unsafe eyrie, in my opinion. She accompanied us to the top, showed us the hand and foot holds, encouraged us, and lent her strong hand over the difficult parts. The symbolism of our helper's name was not lost on us; among other attributes, the goddess Diana is the protector of women (Monaghan 1999:128).

Climbing Bell Rock was, for me, an intense and elegant manifestation of the power of the solar plexus chakra. Afterwards, I felt invigorated for days as any activity that moves energy is beneficial to this chakra. The synergistic combination of physicality and movement of the first two chakras forged an intentional will, which allowed me to approach the summit. I learned something about overcoming inertia–that this is often achieved in cumulative, repeated, small steps, not necessarily by sudden and considerable expenditures of energy. I also discovered that detaching myself from the original intent of climbing the pinnacle and accepting the final outcome, whatever it would be, allowed me to concentrate on the task of the moment–to take the next step. By paying attention to the energy movement in my solar plexus chakra, I balanced my fear and desire of climbing with the need for self-preservation. "Fighting against fear is what we mean by courage." (Peck 1995: 399)

Meditation from the Third Chakra: Through the Fire

This is a standing meditation as the third chakra calls for
energy movement. You have just climbed to the top of a hill or a
height of land. The climb has been more difficult than those you
usually attempt. Relax for a few moments as the breeze cools
your forehead, and your breathing becomes regular. Look back
upon your route and connect with the land you have traversed.

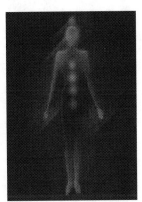

Did she speak to you on your journey?

Standing comfortably with your feet shoulder-width apart, stretch your arms above your
head as you take a deep breath.

Exhaling slowly, bring your arms to your sides, with the palms facing downward. Your
arms extend and elongate as you perform this simple motion.

You are at the centre of the Sun with your arms describing arcs of the Sun's
circumference. As you repeat the movement several times, it feels as if you are pushing
against an unseen force. What is this force your arms encounter? Name it. It is the
impediment that you are working through in your third chakra. Your hands push this
impediment away as Sun's energy erupts from your fingers.

Know that the Sun has blazed for 4.5 billion years and, with your conscious intent, her
energy will help you dissipate any hindrance or hurdle on your
continuing path.

Call upon the energy of Sul, the Sun Goddess, to enter your third
chakra. You have carried this block for many years. Now it is

time to recognize it and put it aside. This may be a difficult task. Perhaps this block has

proven helpful at times.

Perhaps there were times when it furnished a needed defence.

Now, it no longer serves and must be put aside so that your other

gifts and strengths can thrive.

See your sun's energy vapourize the block, scattering its atoms across time and space,

through the cosmos, never to reassemble in your being.

Feel the lightness and the space this release allows into your consciousness.

You feel your consciousness expanding throughout the cosmos.

You are free to explore all the worlds and possibilities previously obstructed.

Where will you go in the Universe and what will you do with this new freedom?

What do you see? Do you choose to explore it?

Remain here for as long as you like, then slowly return your mind to the Orion Galaxy

and the planet called Gaia.

Bring your attention to your present surroundings.

Rest peacefully for a few moments.

Figure 4.2: Sedona Streetscape with Bell Rock in the distance

Figure 4.3: Bell Rock, Sedona, USA

Figure 4.4: Ascending Bell Rock, Sedona, USA
Figure 4.5: Pictographs, Palatki

Chapter V

**The Heart Chakra and Glastonbury Tor,
Glastonbury, England**

In finding what we seek,
We seek what we find.
Travelling the world over,
Do we seek personal truth?
Realize that we must carry it in our heart
or we will find it not.

. . . and there was Glastonbury Tor! I say this with an
exclamation point, because that is the impact; it is
something to behold. . . . From any angle, the Tor
emanates power and mystery. (Bolen 1994:89)

When I first arrived in Glastonbury, my reaction was different from Bolen's. I

was not attracted to the place, after the tranquillity of the Malvern Hills, our previous

destination. Of course, one is awed by the compelling topography, but the air felt

denser and imported a sense of impending discovery, unimagined possibilities that my

rational mind rejected. Definitely too *witchy* for me, I thought. In a few short days, my

view changed completely due to profound healing experiences on the Tor and at Chalice

Well.

Gaia's physical body appears in many forms in the landscape; she lies in the

very Earth as the primordial mother. Caves are her womb; hills are her breasts,

buttocks and pregnant belly; springs are her blood and milk--or her tears. And tears,

symbol of love and compassion, betoken her heart. In Glastonbury, we see the

synthesis of these aspects of Gaia in the cardinal heart chakra.

Anahata, the heart chakra, epitomizes wholeness and compassion, love that is

not dependent upon the qualities of the recipient, the purity of a love which arises from

the individual's recognition of the interconnectedness and interdependence of all things. As the fourth and middle chakra, *Anahata* balances the three lower chakras of the body and the three upper chakras of the mind. A spiral going through each of the chakras begins at the seventh or crown chakra and ends in the heart (Judith 1990: 216). Thus, this chakra is also about relationship, consolidation without constraint. Air, the element associated with this chakra, expresses balance achieved through equalized dispersion and acceptance.

Arising from the lowlands of Somerset, Glastonbury Tor soars to the impressive height of 160 metres above sea level (Devereux 1999: 145). Once an island in an inland sea, the Tor, Celtic for *conical hill*, has been identified with the Isle of Avalon or *Ynis Witrin*, the Isle of Glass and the "crystalline otherworld" (Pennick 2000: 111). The veil between the worlds is thinner here, people say, and it is palpable. This relationship between the worlds of the physical and the cerebral speaks to the heart chakra.

Avalon means "Isle of Apples" (Jones 1996: 31) and small apple orchards, fruit sacred to the goddess, thrive on the flanks of the Tor. Tradition says that maidens, adept in healing arts and the mysteries of creation and death, lived on the Isle. Their names survive as Anu, Danu, Mab, Morrigu, Madron, Mary, Arianrhod, Cerridwen, Rhiannon, Epona, Rigantona, Bride, Brigit, Hecate, Magdalena, Morgana, Gwenhywfar, Vivien and Nimue (Jones 1990: 3). Throughout the centuries, the Tor has also been identified with Gwynn ap Nudd–the Fairy King (Celtic god of the dead), King Arthur, St. Michael and Joseph of Arimathea. Glastonbury, imbued with the power of invoking the distant past, generates and retains a rich mythology of goddess, Arthurian, pre-Christian and Christian lore.

On clear days, the breadth of the low-lying countryside is visible from the summit of the Tor, great sweeps of pasturage and towns sparkle in the sun. A stiff wind is usually present; whipped clouds cast dramatic shadows over the land, with the sun's rays occasionally breaking through in streams of radiance. Misty days invoke the ancient past, when one can easily imagine Glastonbury as an island, the Somerset Plain flooded by sea waters, swirling mists parting to reveal broad marshlands once again.

In addition to its compelling topography, which opens the heart, the Tor's spiral terraces link it to the heart chakra.

The highly visible spiral terraces, contoured in seven concentric rings around the hillside, were probably built between 4000 - 2500 BCE, requiring a considerable degree of social organization and effort. Posited to be a three-dimensional, seven-circuit Cretan labyrinth by Geoffrey Russell, an Arthurian scholar, in 1968, this interpretation met first with scepticism and then conditional acceptance. (Ashe 1979) It is certainly possible to walk the terraces from a starting point, marked by a rock on the southwest face, to the summit; the trek can take between two and five hours. (Mann 1993: 30)

The formation of these steep terraces for agricultural or defensive purposes is considered to be unlikely as the Tor's unfavourable weather exposure renders it inadequate for the former purpose; its lack of space on the summit makes it incapable of containing the population of the surrounding countryside for the latter purpose.

The labyrinth is a physical manifestation of the regenerative path from the outer to the inner world. My personal experience with walking labyrinths is that issues of gratitude, compassion and heart opening come forth. The spiral speaks of growth and change, of death and rebirth, of transformation of consciousness; it is a repetitive pattern that returns us to incrementally deepening considerations of an issue, thus potentiating new understanding and awareness. For me, the labyrinth is also becoming a means of focussing intention and desire with action. The rich combination of walking the labyrinth (doing) in the outer world with reflection (being) in the inner world add purposiveness, or aligning action and meaning.

As the archetype of transformation (Artress 1995:151), the labyrinth on Glastonbury Tor has been used for millennia; indeed, its use continues to the present. With permission gained from the British Heritage Trust, hundreds of people participated in a candle-lit walk up the Tor labyrinth at the turn of this millennium.

Transformation necessarily encompasses birth, whether of new ideas or gifts. The Tor and its surroundings evoke images of birth as the goddess giving birth is personified in the landscape. Her womb is Chalice Hill; the Tor is her breast; her left leg stretches along the length of Wearyall Hill; and the head of the infant, Brigit, emerges as Bride's Mound. (Jones 1996: 19) The potentiality of birth is also actualized by the Tor: "A day or so before childbirth, some expectant mothers have felt a strong urge to climb the Tor and, interestingly, this has heralded the onset of labour." (Howard-Gordon 1982: 9)

In the fall of 1998, I travelled to England with a group of women who would become fast friends and together continue their journeys. Through storytelling, feminist

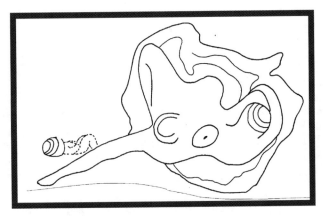

Figure 5.1: Aerial interpretation of contours of Glastonbury Tor showing the mother giving birth

interpretation of history, guided meditations and a past-life regression, a new world opened for me. I began to explore what it means to recapture the divine feminine and to understand with compassion the patriarchal society in which we live. I began to understand the value of the empirical and experiential and to lessen reliance upon the analytical and scientific. All ways of knowing and seeing have their place and time.

Climbing the Tor with my companions, in reverential silence at midnight, was like participating in an ancient procession. The wind lashed clouds across the overcast skies but cleared to reveal a full moon upon our ascent. I felt as if I was being welcomed home. Silently, we walked over the summit and bathed in the moon's glow. There was no need for words. I now use the Tor in grounding meditations by extending a golden cord from my spine to the centre of the Earth and then up through the Earth to the Tor.

As I stand at the summit of the Tor, there is no doubt in my mind that powers and energies beyond our prevailing perceptions exist and that they have an effect in this world. Trusting empirical self-knowledge, without scientific augmentation, is one of the greatest gifts of the heart chakra.

Heart Meditation on a Holy Island

Find something green to sit upon—a blanket or grassy sward. Green is the colour of the

heart chakra and the symbol of Hildegard's "viriditas," the greening power of the affinal

human and the divine. Close your eyes and feel the warm sunshine on your face.

Slowly, a green glow suffuses your heart chakra, extends along your spinal column from

base to crown, and flows down your arms to your hands. Your fingertips tingle as you

allow tendrils of green to eddy from them.

The warmth of the sunlight on your face is interrupted as mists

begin to swirl around you. You hear water lapping at lacustrine

edge and walk toward it, holding your green cloak around you.

At the water's edge, the mists part slightly to reveal a coracle, a

small round boat made of ancient wickerwork and covered with

animal skins.

You step into it and are borne, swiftly and silently, to the Isle of Avalon, the Tor, the

conical hill which reigns over the landscape.

Stepping out of the coracle, you take in the sweeping flanks of the Tor, and its apple

orchards. Are the trees blossoming or bearing fruit? Are they bereft of leaves? You

walk to the southwest edge of the Tor to the stone which marks the entrance of the

labyrinth and begin to walk the spiral to the summit.

What do you observe about yourself, and about the landscape as you walk? How do

you see and know yourself in this landscape?

Have you been here before, in this lifetime, in a past or future one?

This journey to the crest of the Tor is outside of time. You can linger, enjoying the charm of the view, or walk purposefully. Which do you choose?

Whom do you meet along the way? You know that Anu, Danu, Mab, Mary, Arianrhod, Cerridwen, Rhiannon, Brigit, Hecate, Morgana, Gwenhywfar, Vivien and Nimue live and have lived here. Are there other pilgrims or is yours a journey in solitude?

The twists and turns of the labyrinth hold you safely as you take each step of transformation.

And now you have gained the summit. The Somerset Plain extends around you; in the distance are the mountains of Wales. The wind whips the mists, dipping and swirling, as golden shafts of sunlight stream through them.

You become aware of another's presence and turn to greet her. You know who she is, even if you have never encountered her before. She takes your hand and smiles at you

as she fixes you with an unrelenting, yet kindly, gaze. She declaims: "It is with the heart that one can see rightly. What is essential is invisible to the eye. Take my wise words into your heart and know that true sight comes from the heart." You know the certainty of these words with your whole being and are delighted to converse with her. You may ask any question and she will answer from her heart. You may stay here as long as you like.

When you are ready, return to the coracle and your grassy sward.

Figure 5.2: Glastonbury Tor showing the labyrinthine terracing and the Tower of St. Michael.
Figure 5.3: Glastonbury StreetscapeFigure

Figure 5.4: Tower of St. Michael atop the Tor. It is the ruin of a 14th-century church and monastery. Christian churches dedicated to St. Michael were often constructed over hilltop sites sacred to pagan goddesses.

Figure 5.5: Sunlight streams over Somerset Plain; View from Glastonbury Tor.

Chapter VI

The Throat Chakra and the Avebury Complex, England

"The stones have fallen silent," we say.
Monolith, menhir, dolmen, and henge,
Sarsen, cist and stele,
Fogou, quoit, orthostat,
Temenos, tomb, and trilithon,
Capstone, cromlech, kerb and kieve,
Flanker and lintel.
Their names cached beyond human memory,
"The stones have fallen silent," we say
in parody of self-absolution.
But the stones speak when we listen.

The psychological qualities of the base chakras–survival, desire and will–

tempered with the heart's compassion lead us to *Visshudha*, the gateway to

consciousness. In the vibration of the throat chakra, we find our abilities to use voice, to

praise, to truth-tell and to share the deepest expressions of our hearts and minds.

Visshudha potentiates communication, enables us to transcend the individual to connect

and create on a societal level, and activates our recognition of patterns and symbols.

Communication shapes the world as a "symbolic system occupying the meeting

point between the abstract and the manifested idea." (Judith 1990: 262) The element

associated with the throat chakra is ether; likened to breath or spirit, it brings us, both

individually and communally, to the ethereal realm. Sound and vibration, as instruments

of communication, have long been ascribed sacred and generative powers. The

Ancestors of the Australian Aborigines sang the Earth into existence (Abram 1997: 164);

at the beginning of time, Brahman and the Word coexisted, containing one another, the

Vedas say; and the Christian Bible echoes that the World, the Word and

God were coeval and synonymous (Judith 1990: 270).

Vibration with pattern equates to rhythm, an integration profoundly entrained in the Universe, in the Earth, in our physiology and in our consciousness: Once every one hundred thousand years, an emergent attractor in the form of a density wave passes through the spiral galaxies, and in its wake, stars ignite (Swimme 2001); the seasons change annually; once every lunar cycle, women menstruate; and our hearts beat with the Universe.

> At the heart of each of us . . . there exists a silent pulse of perfect rhythm, a complex of wave forms and resonances, which is absolutely individual and unique and yet which connects us to everything in the universe. (Leonard in Judith 1990: 272)

In the throat chakra, we dance the rhythms of communication through which we connect to the past and future in contrast to the lower chakras whose time referent is the present. The dance bridges the present and the past to generate the future. As an analogy of relationships, the dance of communication is a holistic use of symbols with shared meaning to stimulate connection and wholeness within an individual and between individuals in society. With the throat chakra, we engender our future reality.

> The essence of communication is creativity. In the alteration of patterns we become creators, creating the reality and future of our lives at each . . . second. In the fourth chakra we realize that we can control our own evolution–in the fifth chakra we begin doing it. (Judith 1990: 290)

The interdependence of sound, vibration, pattern, rhythm, communication, dance, praise, celebration–all aspects of the throat chakra– correlate to the Neolithic ceremonial complex of Avebury in Wiltshire, England. A few thousand years ago, it was the ritual centre in a landscape of natural elements and monumental earthworks. The complex spreads for kilometres over the chalk downs offering breath-taking panoramas, crop circles, and massive archaeological remains—all the more impressive when one

considers that they were largely constructed using antler picks and rakes, ox scapulae,

and possibly wooden shovels and baskets (Malone 1997: 11). Where archaeologists

have described the site and the marvels of its construction, artist Michael Dames uses

his visual experience to interpret the landscape and its cultural components as the

rostrum of religious rites performed in a yearly cycle. (Gimbutas 1989: 313). Here, in

the third millennium BCE, seasonal rites of life, death and rebirth were enacted in

acknowledgement of the rhythms of nature, and the human interplay with this planetary

reality.

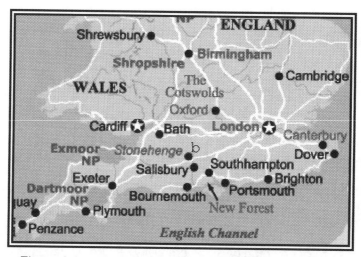

Figure 6.1: Location of Avebury **(b)** inSouthwestern
England

Among other features, the Avebury complex contains the largest stone circle and

henge [ditch] in Europe, remnants of two smaller, interior circles, Silbury Hill, West

Kennett Long Barrow, and two stone avenues, about 2.4 kilometres in length. Other

remains were built by people of the Bronze and Iron Ages, who incorporated or at least

took note of the Neolithic components in siting their own sacred structures in the

landscape. Now, the village of Avebury, occupied since medieval times, and two motor routes bisect the henge and stone circles; sheep graze amongst the sarsens, and the ritual landscape is crossed by roads and fields.

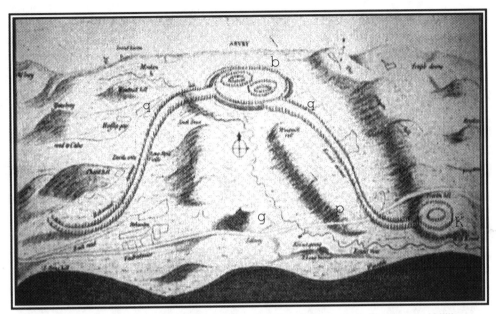

Figure 6.2: The Avebury Complex as drawn by doctor and clergyman William Stukeley in 1743; henge and sarsen circles b, stone rows q, one leading to

In the third millennium BCE, Avebury may have been the most important spiritual centre in Britain with rites taking place at significant times over the year, and the colossal structures represented a living character, Gaia, in each of the four seasons. In February, at a river-side wooden temple, whose ruins are now known as the Sanctuary, puberty rites were acclaimed. On May 1, at the Avebury henge the marriage of the Goddess and her male consort was celebrated; the fertility of their union was consecrated on August Quarter Day at Silbury Hill, the representation of the pregnant goddess in the landscape. Finally, at summer's end, at the burial grounds of West Kennett Long Barrow, the Tomb Lady bade her celebrants to retire under the Earth with her. (Gimbutas 1989:313) Here, in this ancient landscape, are actualized the Womb and the Tomb—both necessary for the continuation of life.

The communal building of these monuments and earthworks, the annual rituals, and the use of the landscape in spiritual rituals as a gateway to a higher consciousness bespeak the throat chakra. "The ritual cycle at Avebury is a vision of cosmic unity and its monumental forms symbolically convey the harmony." (Gadon 1989: 84)

Covering 11.5 hectares with a diameter of 347 metres (Devereux 1992: 124), the henge was probably constructed around 2600 - 2300 BCE (Devereux 1992:126). It has four entrances, still used today by the motor routes; these indicate the ritual nature of the site. The henge, originally ten metres deep but now silted in, encompasses the large circle of stones or sarsens, three to six metres in height—some weighing 40 tonnes, and the remains of what are thought to be two smaller stone circles.

Figure 6.3: Avebury henge and stone circles as they may have appeared 4500 years ago.

Much destruction and reconstruction has occurred over the centuries. Many of the huge sarsens were tumbled and interred in medieval times, perhaps to eradicate their pagan connotation, and in the eighteenth century many were broken for re-use by heating and rapid water-cooling by "Stone Killer Robinson."

Archaeologists estimate that 4000 tons of stone were moved to construct the circles (Devereux 1992: 124), and that people toiled over 1.5 million work hours to dig the henge and circles (Malone 1997: 11).

Silbury Hill, 1.6 kilometres south of the Avebury circles, is the largest, human-made mound in prehistoric Europe, and the focus of this symbolic landscape. Approaching the smaller of the Egyptian pyramids in size, it spirals to a height of 39.5 metres and a diameter of 110 metres. The first of three phases of construction dates to the Late Neolithic, around 2750 BCE. Enigmatic in function from an archaeological perspective, symbolically, it is considered the representation of the pregnant goddess seated in the landscape. The mound itself is the goddess's womb, and her squatting figure is outlined by a surrounding ditch, 14 metres wide and seven metres deep. Until modern medical times, squatting was the preferred posture for giving birth.

With the 1922 excavation of Egyptologist Sir Flinders Petrie failing to confirm the structure's presumed function as a burial site, we are left with the conviction that the hill's symbolism in the landscape, rather than any utilitarian purpose, is the measure through which we may discern its importance, sacredness, and centrality in the lives of its builders. Indeed, it is estimated that 700 people toiled more than ten years to fashion the mound and ditch.

Sophisticated in design, the mound is constructed with horizontal strata of white chalk rubble, cut from the downs, and black turf and soil. A series of spiralling, stepped

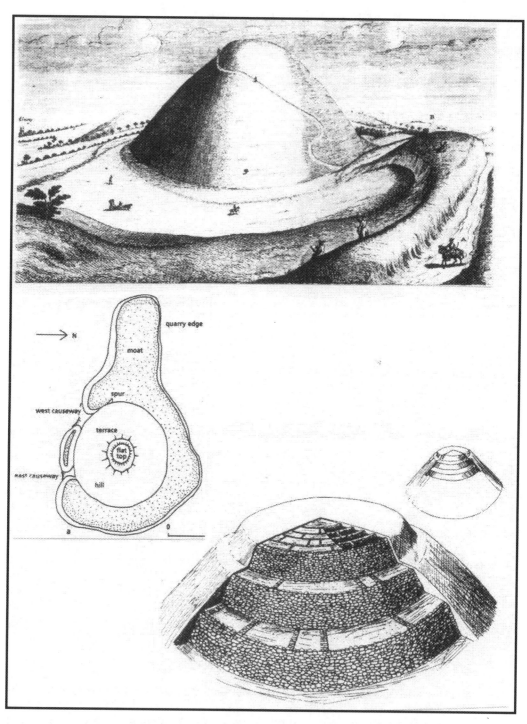

Figure 6.4: Silbury Hill as drawn by William Stukely in 1723 (Malone 1997:22); aerial drawing of Silbury Hill and moat, depicting the Pregnant Goddess (Gimbutas 1989;148); interior stepped construction (Devereux 1992: 129)

walls raise the mound to its impressive height, providing stability over its 4500-year existence. Sightlines from the summit of Silbury to the other Neolithic structures are still discernible and contribute to our present understanding of Silbury Hill as the centre of this symbolic landscape and its attendant rituals.

There are many interpretations of the name "Silbury." "Bury" means hill and "Sil" may be an echo of the Baltic "Saule" or female sun (Devereux 1992: 160, 164), the giver of life, the pregnant goddess, the mother.

The final remarkable feature, West Kennett Long Barrow, lies on a ridge a short distance from Silbury Hill; it was used for more than 1500 years and its earliest phase dates to 3700 BCE (Malone 1997: 29). Lying in an east-west direction, 100 metres long and ten metres high, it is one of Neolithic Britain's largest and best-preserved burial chambers. Only a small segment of the barrow, the first 12 metres, was used for interment and this was plundered extensively in the seventeenth century by a local physician collecting human bones to grind into potions and medicaments. In plan view, a contour map of the long barrow resembles the birth canal. The symbolic significance of burying people, in both primary and secondary burials, within such a mound is to absorb and acknowledge the reality of death's necessary and sacred role in life.

Understanding Avebury as a prehistoric symbolic landscape, where Neolithic peoples connected with an aspect of the Divine, the Earth, brings us to the rediscovery of another gateway of consciousness, lost but not entirely erased in the intervening millennia. It allows us a glimmer of the real, vibrant and complete communion between the Megalith builders and their life-giver, Gaia. "I came to understand that the monuments and their natural environment were indivisible: they were one." (Devereux 1992: 139) With *Visshudha*, the gateway to consciousness we may come to understand the synergy of how ancient peoples existed with and expressed their microcosmic

relationship with the macrocosm.

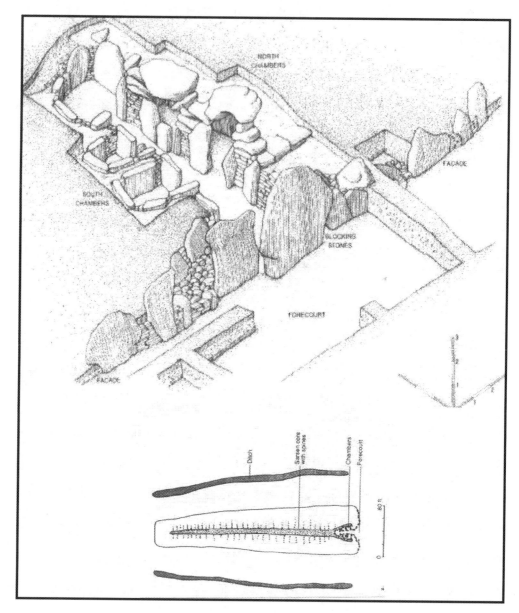

Figure 6.5: West Kennett Long Barrow. A drawing of the burial chambers; and a
contour map showing the feature's resemblance to the birth canal.

Meditation with Chant on Silbury Hill

The warm wind whips your hair, caressing your shoulders, as you sit at the top of

Silbury Hill in the warm glow of Saule, the sun, as she rises on August Quarter Day.

Around you the chalk downs sweep into the distance; the busy motorways and bustling

village fade as the silent, prehistoric landscape reasserts itself.

Slowly turn your head from side to side, as you surveying the avenues of

megaliths, the great henge, the barrow, the green fields. Roll and relax your neck,

preparing for work on your throat chakra,

Draw a deep breath and let your vocal chords vibrate as you exhale.

Softly at first, and then with increasing amplitude, your voice takes wing.

Your throat and chest reverberate.

Open your mouth and let the sound out.

Shape your mouth to make different sounds.

Which sounds are most pleasing to you?

Do they form a mantra?

Listen to the rhythm of your voice.

It is the heartbeat of the Universe.

The whole Universe is entrained to your breathing,

to the rhythm of your breath,

to the pattern of sounds issuing from your throat.

Om

This is the unstruck sound—the sound that is not made by striking

two things together.

Find a mantra by focussing on the sounds your throat

wants to make.

This mantra is a tool to protect your mind from cycling

unproductive thoughts and actions.

You are at the gateway of your consciousness.

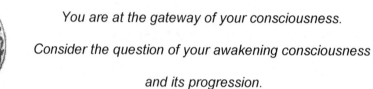

Consider the question of your awakening consciousness

and its progression.

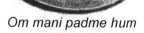

Om mani padme hum

What must you deal with in order to move forward

on your spiritual path?

What truths reside deep in your being?

The time is now ripe to bring them forward.

What do you know about yourself, about the cosmos?

Is the silence as important as the sound?

Sit in silence for a while.

Name and release each thought as it flows through your mind.

When you are ready, thank the Universe for sound and silence.

Figure 6.6: The medieval and modern village of Avebury encroaches on the sarsens.
Figure 6.7: Stone alignment, Avebury, England

Figure 6.8: Henge and sarsens, Avebury, England
Figure 6.9: Silbury Hill, Avebury Complex, England

Chapter VII

The Brow Chakra and Gavrinis, Brittany, France

With my third eye, I spy the seed of my soul
and the edge of the cosmos.
With my third eye, I spy the circle of birth, death,
rebirth and re-death.
With my third eye, I spy the luminous, numinous presence
that is mine, that is yours.
With my third eye, I spy the golden chord,
the harmony of the spheres, the possibility . .
That I am, That is all.
OM Namah Sivaya.

As one accesses the sixth chakra, one espies and reveals one's divinity;

similarly, one reflects the divine within others. With *Ajna,* the brow chakra, "the winged

perceiver," sight takes flight and admits perception with clarity, without duality. Seeing

without eyes, intuiting, is the domain of the brow chakra; when we are able to perceive

or visualize the full scope of life's possibilities, we are then equal to actualizing the

content of these visualizations, to create our reality. In this way, the perceiver becomes

the commander.

The brow chakra is also the seat of clairvoyance, a mystical attribute available to

those who develop it through the intentional synthesis of visualization, memory and

imagination in both waking and dream states. (Judith 1990)

The third eye is related to, but not synonymous with, the brow chakra. This

symbol of the third or spiritual eye, the *Kutastha Chaitanya,* is a

halo encompassing a blue sphere; within it is a five-pointed star,

which represents light and dark. (Fortune8one: ND) It appears in

deep phases of meditation when one is able to perceive with intuition. (Ananada 2001)

Ajna's element is light in all its gradations. Physiologically, dark is simply the absence of light, but psychologically, darkness is often equated with the undesirable. We fear the dark, we lack knowledge of its regenerative workings, and we repudiate its teachings. Yet, it is in the dark that the wonders of the night sky are divulged, and it is with the opening of *Ajna* that we can accept the darkness–to see what *is*, not what *should be,* to accept the spectrum of possibilities.

The ideology of light and dark in our present society is fraught with partiality. We readily embrace that which we consider positive and "of the light" whilst denying the negative or the dark side of matters. This dualistic approach is particularly evident in our treatment of birth and death: The former is usually a joyous, thankful, societal and familial event while the celebratory aspects of the latter are abnegated. Both are equal and central events in any society.

Light and dark, life and death–both physical and metaphysical–are related to the immense tumulus and cairn on the île de Gavrinis, off the coast of Brittany in northwestern France.

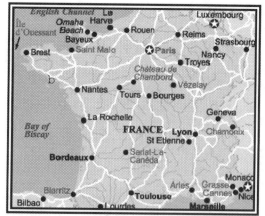

Figure 7.1: Location of Ile de Gavrinis b,
Larmor Baden, Brittany, France

It was built more than five thousand years ago as a monumental tomb and ritual centre. While archaeologists may never be able to interpret the precise nature of the rituals or functions conducted at this megalithic site, we know that it was a tomb, a symbolic representation of the womb and a tribute to the regenerative goddess who subsumes the qualities of light and dark in the process of birth, life, death and rebirth. It seems reasonable to assume that, at Gavrinis, its builders conducted transformative rites and ceremonies embracing these continuations which present society persists in seeing separately.

Built on what was then a peninsula but now an island due to marine inundation, the site is a massive, tiered stone cairn, eight metres high and 50 metres in diameter. It is a remarkable example of Neolithic architecture and art, one of the better preserved monuments of its age in Brittany. A megalithic jamb and lintel provide ingress to the entrance passage (13 metres long) and central chamber (eight metres square) of the cairn. The passage (wide enough for one person) and chamber are lined with huge orthostats. The artwork, meticulously carved on 23 of the 29 orthostats, allows us a window into the past. (Devereux 2001: 25, Le Roux 2001)

Figure 7.2: Drawing of the chambered cairn and tumulus on Gavrinis. The chamber in the centre and its entrance passage are small in comparison to the facade and mound.

Artistically, the rock carvings are of the highest standard. The lineal engravings swirl across the entire face of most of the orthostats in the form of herringbones, hatches, zigzags, croziers (hooks), axes, shields, bows and arrows, serpents, vulvae, concentric semicircles and labyrinths, which lead Gimbutas (1989: 224) to call Gavrinis "the Cathedral of Regeneration." Regeneration subsumes acceptance of life and death, light and dark. The symbolic, artistic unity and repetition of the design elements–their abundance–"seem to say that the creativity of the Goddess is inexhaustible and comes from the cosmic deep." (Gimbutas 1989: 225) For example, Figure 7.3 shows Stone #21. In the centre are glyphs which have been interpreted as axes and identified as symbols of energy. Moreover, these double axes, signifying vulvae and surrounded by flowing, water-like designs, are symbols of the Owl Goddess of Death.

The animal associated with *Ajna* is the owl and the Owl Goddess is well-represented at Gavrinis in the form of engraved hooks, axes, snakes, vulvae, and triangles to name a few. Gimbutas interprets these designs as "life source, energy, or life-stimulating symbols."

> Their association with the Owl Goddess of Death serves to emphasize regeneration as an essential component of her personality. The agony of death which we take for granted is nowhere perceptible in this symbolism. (Gimbutas 1989: 195)

The megalith builders of the Gavrinis cairn seemed to regard the cycle of life, death and regeneration without dualism, as an accepted passage through this reality. The site itself underwent an enactment of the regenerative cycle. There is archaeological evidence which shows that the entrance passage was sealed with ceremony and preceding ritual sometime between 3340 and 2910 BCE (Devereux 2001: 70).

Figure 7.3: Stone #21, showing the double axes (i.e., vulva) within labyrinthine patterns

Figure 7.4: Stone #18 with curvilinear designs and three holes.

One curiously made stone (Figure 7.4) shows curvilinear designs and three holes which converge into one within the rock. When I visited Gavrinis in June of 2001, I placed my hand inside the hole and felt intense cold. My travelling companion experienced the opposite; she later reported that she found the holes to be "very hot with bright red energy" (Stewart: personal communication). Our tour guide explained that geologists and archaeologists had examined the holes and found them to be natural. As an archaeologist, I found that my examination lead me to conclude the opposite, that the holes were not natural and must then be cultural artifact, made by humans. With our current understanding of Neolithic stone carving techniques, we assume that such an endeavour would require great time and energy expenditure.

Evidence of possible use of hallucinogens in the megalithic cultures of western Europe has recently been noted and is coeval with the emergence of the distinctive form of rock art we see at Gavrinis. Was its use related to shamanistic, or spiritual-religious practices? There is "much to be understood about how hallucinogenically altered states of consciousness in ancient times might affect how we should interpret some archaeological sites . . ." (Devereux 2000: 96)

Certain characteristics of *Ajna*–transcending time with memory, using visualization, imagination and dream state to create a new reality–were revealed to me at Gavrinis. I intuited that its peaceful, bucolic aspect contained transformative qualities, which could be incorporated in deep personal healing. I was able to accomplish this in dealing with a difficult interpersonal situation I was experiencing at the time of my visit to Gavrinis. This is what happened.

My trip to Gavrinis was part of a healing holiday in France on which I was travelling with a good friend and two other women whom I had just met. I found the trip difficult because, for no reason I could discern, I had taken an immediate and abiding dislike to one of the women. I will call her Veronica. Travelling in close quarters each day and spending most waking hours together exacerbated my unfounded dislike. I could not shake it or understand it, and I gave this shadow side of myself dominion over much of my personality. I was guarded and unfriendly and could not make myself behave with love and compassion. I could logically and genuinely see many positive aspects of Veronica's character–her charm, effervescence and energy, her care for others, her deep commitment to fairness and respect, her humour and laughter; her love of family. She was an ideal travelling companion in every respect except that I harboured this aversion for which I could not account and which I could not control.

By the time we reached Gavrinis we had been travelling together for several days and I had sunk quite deeply into my shadow. Knowing this could not continue, I agreed to a session of hypnotic past-life regression with my good friend who was leading the journey. As she says, this kind of thing is often about "who killed whom in a past life." (S. Stewart: personal communication) My belief about this practice is pragmatic and open-minded; I neither discount nor rely on it but look to incorporate any useful information it may produce.

The regression revealed that in a past life, in a place I took to be France and a time I took to be the mid-nineteenth century, I had been the older brother to Veronica's younger sister. In her mid-teens, she was passionate, lively and headstrong. My earlier incarnation imagined himself to be her protector and guardian. He brooded about keeping her safe not only through real concern but also from the need of his ego to control. I saw her dancing in a glade of trees, her white dress and long, yellow braid swirling around her, while my incarnation looked on disapprovingly, arms rigidly crossed over chest. Moving a year ahead in time, I saw her funeral. My incarnation's strongest emotion was not sorrow but anger—anger that he had not been able to control her, that Veronica had not followed his dictates, and the result had been her death. Whether this was accurate empirically or only from my earlier incarnate's perspective, I do not know.

Having found a 'reason' for my unreasonable dislike of Veronica, I was able to let it go. I actually felt a huge shift of negative energy. I shared this experience with Veronica and she received it with compassion and forgiveness. Past-life regression is not a replacement or substitution for our present life, but, having undergone the technique twice, I find that the information it supplies is helpful, perhaps crucial, in summoning the forbearance and awareness to deal with a taxing situation. For me, it is the powerful visual and imaginative capacities of the brow chakra which allow such experiences.

Meditation with Ajna

You sit inside the burial chamber on the île de Gavrinis. Though just a stone's throw

away, the brilliant sunshine and lapis waters of the Atlantic Ocean have

joined the kaleidoscope of memories behind your third eye. Encircling and

embracing you are the giant stones whose beautiful, curvilinear symbols,

pregnant with ancient meaning, hold you in darkness. You feel the power

and energy quietly radiating from them and know that this energy is also part of you.

You float complacently, knowing that you are in a womb and a tomb.

In front of you is an earthenware bowl filled with mugwort, star anise, acacia and

saffron. These are the herbal incenses that activate the brow chakra.

You look for a match but cannot find one.

With your eyes closed and focussing the energy of your third eye on the herbs in the

bowl, you soon see a wisp of smoke waft from the bowl

and the herbs' fragrance fills the chamber. Inhale deeply.

From this chamber, you may birth the divine aspects of yourself

that have lain like seeds in your consciousness.

From this chamber, you may travel to distant lands and times, to the outer reaches of

the galaxy, your physical body remaining behind, cradled by the carved rocks,

your third eye fully open and activated.

In the distance, you espy a spark of light. It comes toward you, growing larger.

It is an indigo owl. As she approaches you, she metamorphoses into

human form and you know that she is the Owl Goddess of Death.

You know that she has lived in many forms for eons,

since Gaia birthed the eukaryotes.

This is a comforting and enriching thought.

She is wearing a cloak of many colours which spiral and convolute as you gaze at it.

She beckons you to follow her and leads you to a river where a boatman appears from the swirling rainbow mists.

You board his ferry with trepidation but disembark on the distant shore, knowing that you will find mystery and surcease from fear of both life and death.

The Owl Goddess flies away and leaves you to your discoveries.

You wander along the river's edge and reach a green field where groups of elegantly clothed people discourse in groups of twos and threes. You recognize some of them, your ancestors perhaps, characters from novels, people who have lived and died and made a difference in their worlds. Sit with these people and listen to their stories.

Ask their advice. Stay as long as you like, ask as many questions as you wish.

When you are ready, the Owl Goddess returns, and escorts you across the river, back to the chamber in the centre of the tumulus. You know you have returned to Gavrinis isle as you inhale the robust herbal scents.

Your third eye tingles, as bursts of kaleidoscopic colour flow through your body.

Stay in the darkness as long as you like.

Open your eyes and drink in the beauty of ancient art and knowledge.

Figure 7.5: The passage tomb of Gavrinis, Brittany, France

Figure 7.6: Entrance passage, Gavrinis

Chapter VIII

The Crown Chakra and the Great Pyramid of Khufu, El Giza, Egypt

Ra burns,
burns into my back,
spreading vitality through limbs,
charging and suffusing each cell with white light.

Ra burns as I strain and toil,
inching the granite gargantuan forward with mind and muscle.
Ra burns, as I build the Great Pyramid.

Sahasrara, the crown chakra, contains the potential to achieve a transcendent consciousness in which space and time, paradoxically, conflate and become infinite: where external perceptions are internalized, and where the interconnectedness of all within the Universe is realized. Ancient scholars and contemporary quantum physicists agree that the quintessence of the Universe is consciousness. "The apparently solid things we know through our physical senses are mostly empty space, but what looks empty is really filled with consciousness." (Ardinger 1998: 188) The gift of the crown chakra, the thousand-petaled lotus, brings the possibility of knowing, understanding and connecting to this void as beings of the Universe.

> Within Sahasrara is the full moon . . . resplendent as in a clear sky. It sheds its rays in profusion, and is moist and cool like nectar. Inside it, constantly shining like lightening, is the triangle, and inside this, again, shines the Great Void . . .
> (Avalon in Judith 1990:367)

In the Great Void is All Possibility. Achieving this awareness, whether fleetingly or permanently, is the potential of the crown chakra; here the consciousness of the Great Void–the Cosmic Consciousness–the All-Nourishing Abyss (Swimme 1996: 97)– descends and becomes concrete within one's being while one's consciousness magnifies and flies outward to abstract planes. Undertaking this understanding, Judith (1990: 363) says, is the biggest step because it takes us the farthest, and the smallest, because we are already there. For me, this concept is symbolized by the pyramid whose massive base diminishes to a point of infinite smallness; and conversely, from this microscopic point, expansion to the ends of the Universe is possible. Judith's 1990:92) description of the crown chakra echoes this idea:

> . . . at the final level, chakra seven, our perceptions of the external world are internalized and become once again dimensionless points of focus–pure consciousness–representing symbolically and metaphorically the world around us. At our most transcendental states our consciousness resembles once again the void we began with.

Figure 8.1: Location of the Great Pyramid, El Giza, Egypt [b]

The peak of the pyramid was said to be the meeting place of human and divine beings (Walker 1988: 113); and the word itself in ancient Greek meant "a spirit, thought, symbol or idea of fire" (Walker 1988: 340). It has been speculated that the pyramidal form derives from the visual effect of triangular beams of sunlight radiating through clouds. An entry in the Pyramid Texts, engravings on the walls of burial chambers and corridors of Old Kingdom pyramids, support this idea: "I have laid down for myself this sunshine of yours as a stairway under my feet on which I will ascend . . ." (Harpur 1994:70)

The Great Pyramid of Khufu, the First Wonder of the Ancient World, is the sacred site I associate with the crown chakra. Located on the outskirts of one of the world's most populous cities, it sits serenely and simultaneously in the past and present. I visited Cairo over 20 years ago. I was awestruck simply by the unseen presence of the Great Pyramid on the edge of this fast-paced, disorienting city. As I approached the Giza Plateau through the terrifying Cairo traffic, my amazement was unbounded when the Great Pyramid and its companions appeared through the morning smog–Egyptians bustled by me, seemingly taking no notice of this wonder in their midst. To see such marvels every day of one's life–what must that be like? To go about one's daily activities with the Pyramids of Giza materializing around street corners stretches my imagination; my archaeological sensibilities are barely equal to the task of conceptualizing how Cairenes effortlessly accept the richest symbols of ancient human history and endeavour as part of their daily existence.

Of the man originally entombed in the Great Pyramid, little is known. The Pharaoh Khufu of the Fourth Dynasty of the Old Kingdom, whose image and cartouche appear here, lived over four and a half millennia ago, and reigned from 2551 - 2528 BCE in an age of political confrontation and change; legend says that his tenure was tyrannical. (Baines and Malek 1980: 33-34)

After thousands of years of observation and study, much is known about the Great Pyramid, and even more is conjectured.. Although the stones themselves are silent, historians, archaeologists, archaeoastronomers, metaphysicians, geometers

and pyramidologists have waxed eloquently on their behalf. They estimate that the funerary monument was constructed with 2,300,000 granite or limestone blocks, each with a weight of about 2.5 tons and a collective mass of 5.75 million tons, a feat made even more considerable as it was accomplished without the use of the pulley or wheeled vehicles. Its height of just under 150 metres was surpassed only at the beginning of the last century. Dozens of mathematical correlations between the measurements of the Great Pyramid with astronomic and geomantic alignments have been noted, and their significance discussed for centuries; for example, the relationship between the height of the Great Pyramid in metres, the polar radius of the Earth and the distance between the Earth and sun at perihelion in millions of kilometres. (Moroney 1994, CNN 2001) The pyramid's casing of white Turah limestone–imagine how this must have blazed in the desert sun–is now missing, as is its eight-metre high enclosure. Although the Great Pyramid has furnished building materials for much of old Cairo and Giza, it remains virtually indestructible. An Arab proverb says: "Man fears Time, yet Time fears the Pyramids" (Ashmawy 2001); as symbols of eternity, they are unequalled.

Intended as permanent and immutable funerary monuments, it is ironic that the pyramids also became centres for recycling wealth. Robbers removed riches from the tombs and reinserted them into economic circulation. Also paradoxical is the idea that while most of the population believed in an afterlife provided with material treasures, many must also have braved the social and religious sanctions against their disturbance to desecrate these tombs.

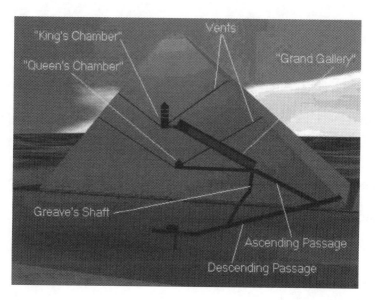

An explanation of the mystery that resulted in the manifestation of the Universe is that it was created from the Great Void by Spirit moving in specific geometric patterns. These patterns, actualized as Sacred Geometry, explicate our relationship to the Universe; further they appear in the geometry of nature and in human constructs such as buildings and structures. Two of these patterns are amongst many reflected in the construction of the Great Pyramid. The first is the Golden Ratio, a universal mode linking natural phenomena with mathematics, music, and art and architecture. It is reflected in sunflowers, spiral shells, the proportions of the human body, DNA, quasi-crystals, viruses, vibrations, etc.. Pictured here, the Golden Ratio is a proportion determined by dividing a line into two unequal parts such that the shorter section relates to the longer section as the longer relates to the entire line. The Golden Ratio is marked as the letter Φ and expressed numerically as 1 : 1.618. It is named after Phidias, Greek sculptor and artistic director of the construction of the Parthenon. (Fletcher 1995:1; Calter 1998) Symbolically, the Golden Ratio pertains to the Golden Mean, the

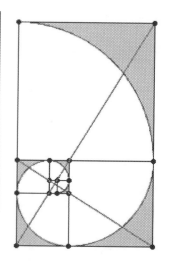

principle of moderation of Greek and Roman philosophy. This relates to *Sahasrara,* the crown

chakra, in that balancing the energies of the first six chakras allows one to reach transcendent

levels.

Also encoded within the proportions of the Great Pyramid is the geometric process of

squaring the circle, that is constructing a square whose area equals that of a given circle, or a

square whose perimeter equals the perimeter of a given circle. Impossible to solve on paper using

only a straightedge and compass, the ancient Egyptians may have used a method that

incorporates this precept.

> Take a wheel of any diameter and lay out a square base one revolution on a
> side. Then make the pyramid height equal to two diameters. By this simple
> means you get a pyramid having the exact shape of the Great Pyramid
> containing perimeter-squaring of the circle and area squaring of the circle
> and . . . the golden ratio! (Calter 1998)

Symbolically, the square represents earthly things, while the circle represents the divine.

Squaring the circle may be interpreted as a universal metaphor for bringing the earthly into a

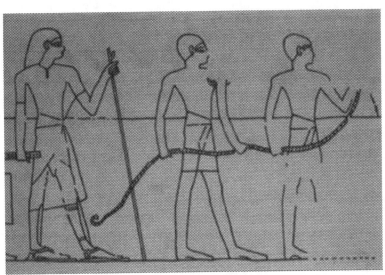

congruent affiliation with the divine, the teaching of *Sahasrara.*

As symbols of ancient Egypt, the pyramids represent early expressions of astute ideas: A world view "based upon the actual quest to make the world one, to establish the interconnection of all things, to reconstruct the universe as it was in the beginning." (Asante 2000: 3)

Meditation to Join the Universe

Gently stretch and sit on a multi-coloured cushion. In your mind's eye,

you sit at the top of the Great Pyramid of Khufu, the limitless desert sands

stretching to the south into the ancient past.

Behind you is the frenetic activity of modern Cairo.

Simultaneously, you absorb the sounds of the city and the silence of the

desert, allowing each to enter your consciousness, taking note of their

intricacies and letting them go. Remain here for a while, as the desert shimmers and the

kaleidoscopic passing of millennia culminate in this moment.

Inhale as you draw the colour of glowing red to Muladhara, your root chakra. It suffuses the base

of your spine with warmth.

Know that you are safe, that you belong, that you are wanted and beloved; the joy of

belonging is yours.

Accept this knowledge and embody it. Accept the mystery and wonder of your being

and of all beings.

Remain here as long as you wish.

When you are ready, inhale as you draw the colour of passionate orange up through your root

chakra to Svadhisthana, your sacral chakra. Know that your sensuality

and physicality are dynamic and respected parts of you through which you

interact consciously with others in divine relationship.

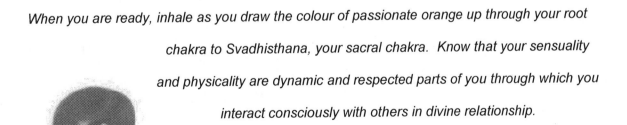

Inhale as you draw up the colour of solar yellow to Manipura, your third chakra. Know that this is your centre, that it contains your considerable power and gentleness, that you possess boundless courage and compassion.

The gifts of your base chakras are unique and necessary to the continued unfolding of the universe and its mystery, of which you are an integral part.

Inhale as you draw verdant, iridescent green to Anahata, your heart chakra. Here the strengths of your three lower and upper chakras are balanced with compassion and love–love for oneself; for two-leggeds; for four-leggeds; for stationary beings; for the stone entities whose faces remain unchanged through eons, taking epochs to crack a smile; for Gaia, the planetary being, who is the centre of the Great Mystery; for the galaxies and astronomical beings who contain the Great Possibility, encapsulated in your being.
Know that the Universe created your being to embody the power of love; the Universe is Love and Love existed before the Great Flaring Forth.
With love all is possible.

Inhale and draw the colour of sapphire blue to Vissudha, your throat chakra. Understand that all ideas, opinions, manifestations, prophecies, truths are possible and desirable.
Here you traverse the razor's keen edge, as you elegantly acknowledge, without contradiction, both paradox and dualism.

Inhale and draw the colour of deep indigo to Ajna, your brow chakra. You see *with clarity and wisdom, with senses not yet named. You seek only the truth.*

Inhale and draw the colour of misty amethyst to

Sahasrara, your crown chakra.

You see the sacredness of the present moment and know that this moment exists throughout

space, throughout time. You are a part of the space/time

continuum, the Cosmic Consciousness. Look along your

lifetime, your many lifetimes, and see the multitude of

infinitesimally small steps you have taken. Look along your

unlived lives. You exist as pure thought, even as you feel the

energies resonating throughout your chakras.

The colours and vibrations of your chakras commingle into white light.

They swirl above, below and all around you.

Imagine the thousand-petaled white lotus of Sahasrara

blossoms at your crown.

You and the Divine are one.

Touch her face, she awaits your precious being.

You and Gaia are one.

Feel her breath stir the hot desert air around you.

You and the Universe are one.

Feel the vastness of the cosmos inside your body.

Know.

Share this knowledge in joyous communion with all beings around the world.

Figure 8.2: The Pyramids of Giza from modern Cairo
Figure 8.3: Three pyramids and the Sphinx

Figure 8.4: The Pyramid of Khufu

Figure 8.5:The Pyramid of Khephren (2520 - 2494 BCE) at El Giza, son and eventual successor of Khufu, showing the overlay of Turah limestone still adhering to the peak.

Chapter IX

IN THE END IS THE BEGINNING

End
Finite, terminal
Grieving, cleaving, completing
The end begins.
Beginning.

While spiritual practices such as meditation and prayer may take one to altered levels of awareness, being with the Earth in its natural beauty and sacred heritage is an equally dynamic tool for integrating experience and expanding consciousness. The outward or physical journey to a sacred place is the manifestation of the inward journey. To me, travel to sacred sites is a necessary part of my spiritual path, enriching and enhancing other ways of learning and knowing.

> When we travel from our own country to experience
> sacred places in other lands we act as bees bringing
> pollen from one plant to another so that the plant species
> can continue to live. We bring our knowledge from one
> culture to another, and we take back with us experiences
> we can then apply to our own lives and society. . . . Just
> as bees carry pollen from plant to plant, so migratory
> humans carry spiritual ideas and experiences from one
> land to another. . . . The value of cross-pollination is to
> see things in a fresh way. (Pollack 1997: 51)

In this thesis, I have explored relationships between the seven major chakras and seven places, which I consider to be examples of sacred heritage. I have suggested that using the energies of one's body and Gaia's body in meditation at these places may open one to experiences and alternate ways of knowing and connecting with oneself, other beings, the Earth, and the Universe. Prime moments of spiritual growth are frequently associated with sacred places.

Figure 9.1: Nature and Art

"Landscape and nature know us and the returning echo seems to confirm that we belong here." (O'Donohue 1999: xxi)

Over the course of the past few centuries, Western society has come to extol the objective rather than the subjective avenue as the authoritative way of acquiring knowledge; the subjective approach was abjured in a society that valued formal acquisition of knowledge over the experiential. Now, the validity of seeking information and answers internally and with the senses has re-emerged. With our current understanding of our groundedness in the very sensuality and physicality of earthly existence, we admit the appropriateness of accepting the knowledge of body, mind and spirit. The paradox seems to be that objectivity is intrinsically rooted in our subjective wisdom. Abram's (1997: 34) exquisite words show this: "Our spontaneous experience of the world, charged with subjective, emotional, and intuitive content, remains the vital and dark background of all our objectivity."

Using the chakras as a means of acquiring subjective knowledge about oneself and one's interconnection with the Universe is a valid and increasing valuable endeavour.

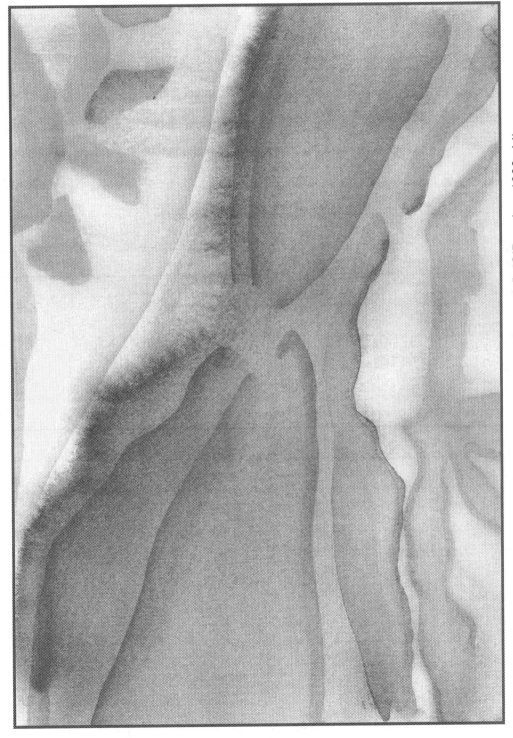

Figure 9.2: Art and Nature "We belong on the earth." (O'Donohue 1999: 14)

APPENDIX A: ATTRIBUTES OF THE SEVEN MAJOR CHAKRAS

	1: Muladhara	2: Svadisthana	3: Manipura	4: Anahata	5: Visuddha	6: Ajna	7: Sahasrara
Associated system (Schultz 1998)	blood and bones	sex organs and lower back	solar plexus, GI tract	heart, lungs, thymus	throat, thyroid and neck	third eye, brain pituitary	crown, muscles, connective tissue
Associated organ (Swan 1990)	sexual glands	spleen	pancreas	thymus gland	thyroid	pituitary gland	pineal gland
Associated endocrine gland (Judith 1997)	testicles or adrenals	ovaries, testicles	adrenals, pancreas	thymus	thyroid, parathyroid	pineal	pituitary
Colour	deep red	orange	yellow	green	cerulean blue	indigo	violet
Planet (Johari 1987)	Mars	Mercury	Sun	Venus	Jupiter	Saturn	Ketu
Planet (Judith 1997)	Saturn, Earth	Moon	Mars, Sun	Venus	Mercury, Neptune	Jupiter	Uranus
Season	winter	spring	summer	fall			
Musical note	C	D	E	F sharp	G	A	B flat
Associated verb (Judith 1997)	I have	I feel	I can	I love	I speak	I see	I know
Number of lotus petals	4	6	10	12	16	2	1000

	1: Muladhara	2: Svadisthana	3: Manipura	4: Anahata	5: Visuddha	6: Ajna	7: Sahasrara
Substance (Redmond 1997)	earth	water	fire	air	ether	unified field of pure light	realm of pure light; enlightened consciousness of ultimate reality; altar where goddess and god unite in orgasm of healing, expanding and uplifting energy
Mythic images (Swan 1990)	dragon, ape, bull, business, elephant, whale	eros, lovers, rabbit, moon, art	ram, shark, will to power	mother and child, love, alchemist's gold	hero, mountain goat, explorer	scholar, skull, wise people, owl, eagle	crystal, star, mountain peak, angel
Goddess (Ardinger 1998)	Baba Yaga (Slavic)	Hathor (Egyptian)	Oya (Afro-Brazilian)	Kuan Yin (Chinese)	Sarasvati (Hindu)	Cumaean Sybil (Greco-Roman)	Sophia (Gnostic)
Force (Judith 1990)	gravity	attraction of opposites	combustion	equilibrium	sympathetic vibration		
Seed sound (Judith 1990)	LAM	VAM	RAM	YAM / SAM	HAM	OM	None as yet
Vowel sound (Judith 1990)	O as in Om	U as in Oo	A as in Ah	E as in Ay	I as in Ee	mm or nn	nng or silence

APPENDIX B: THE CHAKRA SYSTEM AS ORGANIZING CONSTRUCT

	1: Muladhara [Root Support]	2: Svadisthana [Her Special Abode or Dwelling Place of the Self]	3: Manipura [City of Shining Jewel]	4: Anahata [Not Struck]	5: Visuddha [Purified]	6: Ajna [Command]	7: Sahasrara [Thousand-petalled or Unqualified Absolute]
Campbell 1974	world view is uninspired materialism; psychologically reactive, not active; propensity to hoard and guard things; hanging on to existence	aim of life is in sex and sexual energies; recognize and affirm importance of this centre to allow energies to pass through and transform	heat and light; energy turns to violence and its aim is to master; "will to power;"	the place where the sound is heard "that is not made by any two things striking together," such a sound is the creative energy of the Universe, the hum of the void, the precipitate; here the Great Self lives and portals open to the void	once the sound has been heard and the mystery acknowledged, desire is to know it more fully; threshold of embarkation for the Land of No Return. "It is the sharpened edge of a razor, hard to traverse."	conditioned rapture; first degree of illumination once the tasks of the fifth chakra have been accomplished	unconditioned rapture; "Man's last and highest leave-taking is the leaving of God for God." (Meister Eckhart); our god and our selves explode into light, beyond thought and experience
Swan 1990	power and pleasure	creativity, sex, emotions	assertion, community	love, compassion, great virtues	will, expression, communication	thinking, decision-making	spirituality, integration

	1: Muladhara [Root Support]	2:Svadisthana [Her Special Abode or Dwelling Place of the Self]	3: Manipura [City of Shining Jewel]	4: Anahata [Not Struck]	5: Visuddha [Purified]	6: Ajna [Perceive, Command]	7: Sahasrara [Thousand-petalled or Unqualified Absolute]
Northrup 1994	is affected by how secure and safe we feel in the world	contains stored memories, emotions and information about how we relate to others	associated with self-esteem, self confidence and self-respect	symbolic of self-love and ability to feel unconditional love	power of will, communication, personal expression, following one's dreams	related to personal vision, knowledge, intuitive sills, self-evaluation and introspection	related to seeing the larger purpose in our lives; related to attitudes of faith, values, ethics, courage and humanitarianism
Judith ND	earth; physical identity; survival	water; emotional identity, sex	fire; ego identity, power	air; social identity, love	sound; creative identity, communication	light; archetypal identity, vision	thought; universal identity, understanding
Endicott 1994	tests of security	tests of sexuality and desires	tests of power and will	tests of love	tests of expressing one's truth	tests of vision	tests of faith
Schultz 1998	Physical Safety, security, support in the world; sense of self, independence; self-sufficiency; fearlessness; trust	Relationships and drive; well-defined boundaries; creation and creativity; partnership and healing; relationships and boundaries	Responsibility and self-esteem; degree of competence, ambition, assertion; gut feelings; commitment; who am I?	Emotions, intimacy, nurturance; power and vulnerability; who am I at heart?	Communication, timing and will; determination; resilience; creativity	Perception, thought and morality; focus; balance wisdom and knowledge against ignorance; rigidity/flexibility; linear/non-linear;	A Purpose in Life; why am I here?; the divine and I are one; maintain a sense of purpose but accept some uncertainty; locus of control and creation
Ardinger 1998	physical health, right livelihood, prosperity, grounding, survival	pleasure, sexuality, emotions, social issues	strength of will, sense of purpose, vitality	compassion, self acceptance, balance in relationships	clear communication, self-expression, creativity	imagination, intuition, psychic perception	knowing, understanding, connecting

Judith 1997						
survival and grounding; stillness, firmness and stability; associated with Gaia, Demeter; four petals reflect the four elements of the material kingdom	consciousness thrives on change; dragon represents consuming passion which must be harnessed to progress; desires lead to movement and change; emotions, sexuality, nurturance, clairsentience; empathy	metabolism, combustion, power; energy-dance of matter and movement; first level of intellect; power of life, combination, vitality and interaction; *yang* and active; ability to overcome patterns of inertia; combines polarity to create wholeness; appreciating diversity; will is the combination of mind and action	"eye of the hurricane;" we embrace the larger pattern, and play our part in the web; integrates and balances mind and body; sense of wholeness; centre of love; love is no longer dependent; relationship; affinity with others and composite parts of self; experience of love as an infinite source	gateway to consciousness; communication organizes and expands consciousness; sound has a purifying nature; Hindus believe that matter was created from vibration; mantras entrain a vibration which creates greater order and harmony; through creativity the mysteries of the Universe are opened; transcends space	darkness and light intertwined; psychic communication; transcends time; clairvoyant seeing as a willed process of visualization developed through memory, visualization and imagination; command-creation of reality through the projection of our visualizations; transcends time with memory, visualization, dream state; timeless dimension	centre of cosmic consciousness or awareness of a cosmic order; represents our belief systems which rule our actions with harmony, not domination; considered by the Hindus to be the seat of enlightenment; element is thought and function is knowing; access of knowledge from within; nature of consciousness is to manifest and liberate; has both cognitive and transcendent consciousness; self-conscious evolution; enlightenment means cumulative steps of accepting understanding over ignorance

	1: Muladhara [Root Support]	2: Svadisthana [Her Special Abode or Dwelling Place of the Self]	3: Manipura [City of Shining Jewel]	4: Anahata [Not Struck]	5: Visuddha [Purified]	6: Ajna [Command]	7: Sahasrara [Thousand-petalled or Unqualified Absolute]
Owlsdottir ND	The right to exist, care for oneself, have possessions	The right to feel, to express and understand one's emotions, needs, and wants	The right to act, to be innovative and free	The right to love and be loved: freedom from prejudice, low self-esteem, and violent conflict. If another right is harmed, the right to love may also be harmed.	The right to speak and hear truth: to be heard, and to voice one's knowledge.	The right to see: to perceive accurately, to realize the scope of one's vision.	The right to know: the right to truth, accurate information. This includes spiritual knowledge and the right to interpret the divine.
LeBrun 1997	Logical Level of Environment: [Where and When]. There is a logical connection between the earth element and the experience of personal, physical surroundings.	Logical Level of Behaviours: [What]. Driven by emotional state and related to condition of resourcefulness.	Logical Level of Capability: [How]. The ability to take action. One's capability forms the channel through which this energy can flow.	Logical Level of Beliefs, Values, Attitudes [Why]. Centre of identity-who I think I am.	Logical Level of Choice [Which]. Associated with sound which represents verbal and written manifestations of how we make our presence felt in the world.	Logical Level of Identity [Who]. With the third eye we see beyond the present reality to possibilities.	Logical Level of Spirituality [Who Else?] Where we connect to something greater than corporeal reality.

	1: Muladhara [Root Support]	2: Svadisthana [Her Special Abode or Dwelling Place of the Self]	3: Manipura [City of Shining Jewel]	4: Anahata [Not Struck]	5: Visuddha [Purified]	6: Ajna [Command]	7: Sahasrara [Thousand-petalled or Unqualified Absolute]
Myss 1996	Tribe: archetype of group identity, group willpower, group belief patterns; grounding; sense of safety and connection to physical world; sacred truth is "All is One."	Power: partnership, need for relationships with others; need to control dynamics of physical environment; energy generates sense of personal identity and psychological boundaries; spiritual challenge is to learn to interact consciously with others; sacred truth is "Honour one another."	Self: personal power in relation to external world; self-esteem; sacred truth is "Honour oneself."	Love: emotional power; mediates between body and spirit; most powerful energy we have is love; resonates to emotional perceptions; capacity to "let go and let god;" release emotional pain to reach tranquillity; forgiveness; release need for self-determined justice; inspiration, hope, trust; ability to heal oneself and others; sacred truth is "Love is the divine power."	Will: release of personal will to divine choice; power of choice; faith, self-knowledge, personal authority; decision-making; centre of choice and spiritual karma; personal power lies in thoughts and attitudes; sacred truth is "Surrender personal will to divine will."	Clarity: power of the mind; wisdom, intuitive sight; opening the mind; developing an impersonal mind; retrieving one's power from 'false' truths; acting on internal direction; discriminating between thoughts motivated by fear or strength; wisdom acquired through life experiences and detachment of impersonal mind; separate truth from illusion; sacred truth is "Seek only the truth."	Transcendence: spiritual connector; capacity to allow spirituality to become integral part of life and guidance; contains purest form of energy, grace, prana; mystical realm; dimension of conscious rapport with the divine; sacred truth is "Live in the present moment."

	1: Muladhara [Root Support]	2: Svadisthana [Her Special Abode or Dwelling Place of the Self]	3: Manipura [City of Shining Jewel]	4: Anahata [Not Struck]	5: Visuddha [Purified]	6: Ajna [Command]	7: Sahasrara [Thousand-petalled or Unqualified Absolute]
Fox 1999	Cosmology: firelessness; all other chakras depend on this base chakra to be engaged and alive, open and flowing; grounding; indigenous dance is based on awareness of first chakra; associated with vibratory energy and cosmology; spiritual journey begins with sound. Blessings of sounds and vibrations.	Feminist Philosophy: passion, lust, yearning for union of all kinds; generative fire; sexual chakra;; power to beget, conceive and give birth; corresponds to feminist philosophy; overcoming dualism; living life of interconnectivity Blessings of sensual and sexual self.	Liberation: power, anger; place of chi and centring; place of strength and empowerment; corresponds to liberation theology; compassion and moral outrage begin here; justice-making is important expression. Blessings of gut reactions, anger, journey to empowerment for self and others.	Compassion: culmination of passions in the fire of love; begin with the heart; centre of body; *viriditas*; prana (divine energy force) resides in the heart; connected to breath (lungs); forgiveness; self-liberation. Blessings of heart and immune system, defences and circulatory system.	Prophecy: truth-telling; sharing fires lit in our hearts and minds; door; expressing one's truth and wisdom. Blessings of singing, speaking, praising oneself and others.	Creativity: wisdom; joining of intellect and intuition; third eye; fires of creativity, hope, intuition; perception; mid-ground between brain hemispheres; balance of synthetic and analytical work. Blessings of mind, study, learning and creativity.	Community: emits fire and sends light waves into Universe to connect with other light beings. Blessings of warmth, light gravity and light - connecting, community - making, diversity and ecumenism.

	1: Muladhara [Root Support]	2: Svadisthana [Her Special Abode or Dwelling Place of the Self]	3: Manipura [City of Shining Jewel]	4: Anahata [Not Struck]	5: Visuddha [Purified]	6: Ajna [Command]	7: Sahasrara [Thousand-petalled or Unqualified Absolute]
Jung ND	conscious world; people are victims of impulses, instincts, un-consciousness	psychic life begins	centre of emotions; the fire of passion, wishes and illusions	here is the purusa, a small figure that is the divine self, namely that which is not identical with causality, nature or a mere release of energy; individuation begins; self is impersonal and objective; the prospective spirit is born and starts becoming conscious	a full recognition of the psychical essences the fundamental essences of the world; psychical reality; sphere of abstraction	the subtle body develops; the divine is fully awakened	plane of transcendence

SELECTED BIBLIOGRAPHY

Abram, David. The Spell of the Sensuous: Perception and Language in a More-than-Human World. New York: Vintage Books, 1997.

Ananda. Joy is Within You!: The Spiritual Eye. December 6, 2001. http://www.anandaseattle.org/SpiritualEye.htm (December 17, 2001)

Ardinger, Barbara. Goddess Meditations. St. Paul, Minnesota: Llewellyn Publications, 1998.

Artress, Lauren. Walking a Sacred Path: Rediscovering the Labyrinth as a Spiritual Tool. New York: Riverhead Books, 1995.

Asante, Moelfi Kete. The Egyptian Philosophers: Ancient African Voices from Imhotep to Akhenaton. Chicago, Illinois: African American Images, 2000.

Ashe, Geoffrey. The Glastonbury Tor Maze. Glastonbury: Gothic Image Publications, 1979.

Ashmawy. Alaa K. "The Great Pyramid of Giza." 2001. http://ce.eng.usf.edu/pharos/wonders/pyramid.html. (February 16, 2002)

Baines, John and Jaromir Malek. Atlas of Ancient Egypt. New York: Facts on File Publications, 1980.

Bayuk, Andrew. "Khufu." Guardian's Egypt. 2002. http://www.guardians.net/egypt/khufu.htm (February 15, 2002).

Berry, Thomas. The Great Work: Our Way into the Future. New York: Bell Tower, 1999.

Bertulli, Margaret. "The Franklin Mystery." Northern Vignettes. ND. Prince of Wales Northern Heritage Centre, Yellowknife, Northwest Territories, Canada. http://www.pwnhc.ca/exhibits/nv/franklin.htm. (November 11, 2001).

Bolen, Jean Shinoda. Crossing to Avalon: A Woman's Mid-Life Pilgrimage. San Francisco: HarperCollins, 1994.

Brockman, Norbert C. Encyclopedia of Sacred Places. New York: Oxford University Press, 1998.

Calter, Paul. The Golden Ratio and Squaring the Circle in the Great Pyramid. 1998. http://www.dartmouth.edu/~matc/math5.geometry/unit2/unit2.html. (March 3, 2002).

Campbell, Joseph. The Mythic Image. Princeton, New Jersey: Princeton University Press, 1974.

Canadian Museum of Civilization. Life and Art of an Ancient Arctic People. ND. http://www.civilization.ca/archeo/paleoesq/ped01eng.html. (November 6, 2001).

"Chalice Well Gardens." ND. http://www.chalicewell.org.uk/home.html (November 13, 2001).

Coe, William R. Tikal. Philadelphia: The University Museum, University of Pennsylvania, 1977.

Coon, Robert. "Earth Chakras." 2001. http://www.geocities.com/earthchakras/sacred_sites.html . (February 17, 2002).

CNN. "Sun heats up Earth in long distance relationship." July 5, 2001. http://www.cnn.com/2001/TECH/space/07/04/sun.distant/. (February 16, 2002)

Devereux, Paul. Symbolic Landscapes: The Dreamtime Earth and Avebury's Open Secrets. Glastonbury, England: Gothic Image Publications, 1992.

The Illustrated Encyclopedia of Ancient Earth Mysteries. London: Cassell and Co., 2000.

Dreaming the Earth," Symbolic Landscapes. http://www.gothicimage.co.uk/books/symboliclands1.html. 2001 (August 2001).

Places of Power: Measuring the Secret Energy of Ancient Sites. London: Cassell,

1999.

Endicott, Gwendolyn. The Spinning Wheel: The Art of Mythmaking. Portland, Oregon: Attic
        Press, 1994.

Fletcher, Rachel. Harmony by Design: The Golden Mean as a Design Tool. New York:
        Beverly Russell Enterprises, 1995.

Fortune8one. "The Pentacle." http://www3.telus.net/fortune8one/. ND. (December 18,
        2001).

Fox, Matthew. Sins of the Spirit, Blessings of the Flesh: Lessons for Transforming Evil in
        Soul and Society. New York: Three Rivers Press, 1999.

Gadon, Elinor W. The Once and Future Goddess: A Symbol for Our Time. San Francisco:
        HarperCollins, 1989.

"Gaian Theories." http://www.crystalinks.com/gaia.html. ND. (October 27, 2001).

Gimbutas, Marija. The Language of the Goddess: Unearthing the Hidden Symbols of
        Western Civilization. London: Thames and Hudson, 1989.

Graves, Tom. Needles of Stone. http://www.isleofavalon.co.uk/ndlstone.html, 1998.

Griffyn, Sally. Sacred Journeys: Stone Circles and Pagan Paths. London: Kyle Cathie
        Limited, 2000.

Hardcastle, F. The Chalice Well, Glastonbury, Somerset, England: A Short History.
        Somerset: The Chalice Well Trust, 1990.

Harpur, James. The Atlas of Sacred Places: Meeting Points of Heaven and Earth. New
        York: Henry Holt and Company, 1994.

Henderson, Joseph L. "Ancient Myths and Modern Man." In Man and His Symbols by Carl
        G. Jung. New York: Dell Publishing Company, 1979.

Howard-Gordon, Frances. Glastonbury: Maker of Myths. Exeter: Sydney Lee Limited, 1982.

Jaffe, Matthew. "Beyond the Bounds of Sedona." Sunset, April 1996.
    http://www.findarticles.com. (November 25, 2001).

Johari, Harish. Chakras: Energy Centers of Transformation. Rochester, Vermont: Destiny
    Books, 1987.

Jones, Kathy. The Goddess in Glastonbury. Glastonbury, England: Ariadne Publications,
    1990.

Judith, Anodea. Wheels of Life: A User's Guide to the Chakra System. St. Paul, Minnesota:
    Llewellyn Publications, 1990.

    "The Chakra System." http://www.sacredcenters.com/, N.D. (March 3, 2002).

Jung, C. G. "Jung on the Chakras." ND. The Psychology of Kundalini Yoga.
    http://www.lightmind.com/jung/seminar/chakras.html. (March 3, 2002).

Keenleyside, Ann, Margaret Bertulli and Henry Fricke. "The Final Days of the Franklin
    Expedition: New Skeletal Evidence". Arctic 50(1):36-46, 1997

LeBrun, Louise. Levels of Thinking and the Chakras.
    http://www.partnersinrenewal.com/chakras.htm. 1997. (October 28 2001).

Le Roux, Charles-Tanguy. Carnac, Locmariaquer and Gavrinis. Rennes, France: Éditions
    Ouest-France, 2001.

Lovelock, James. The Ages of Gaia: A Biography of our Living Earth. New York: W. W.
    Norton and Company, 1988.

Malone, Caroline. The Prehistoric Monuments of Avebury. London: English Heritage, 1997.

Mann, Nicholas. Glastonbury Tor: A Guide to the History and Legends. Butleigh, England:
    Triskele Publications, 1993.

McGhee, Robert. "Signs and Symbols of an Ancient People: The Dorset Palaeo-Eskimos of
    Brooman Point." July 20, 2001.
    http://www.civilization.ca/cmc/archeo/oracles/brooman/52.htm (November 9, 2001).

Michell, Paul. New Light on the Ancient Mystery of Glastonbury. Glastonbury, England: Gothic Image Publications, 1997.

Monaghan, Patricia. The Goddess Path: Myths, Invocations and Rituals." St. Paul, Minnesota: Llewellyn Publications, 2000.

Moroney, Alison. "Giza Master Plan." 1994. http://members.optusnet.com.au/~astrology11/giza.html. (February 16, 2002).

Myss, Caroline. Anatomy of the Spirit: The Seven Stages of Power and Healing. New York: Three Rivers Press, 1996.

Naropa. "Ten Principals of Creation Spirituality." 2001. http://www.creationspirituality.org/faqs.html#WhatCS. (February 18, 2002).

Northrup, Christiane. Women's Bodies, Women's Wisdom: Creating Physical and Emotional Health and Healing. New York: Bantam Books, 1994.

O'Donohue, John. Anam Cara: A Book of Celtic Wisdom. New York: HarperCollins Publishers, 1998.

Eternal Echos: Celtic Reflections on our Yearning to Belong. HarperPerennial, 1999.

Osmen, Sarah Ann. Sacred Places. New York: St. Martin's Press, 1990.

Owlsdottir, Freya. Chakras. http://www.owlsdottir.com/chakras/chakras.html. ND. (October 27, 2001).

Pennick, Nigel. Celtic Sacred Landscapes. New York: Thames and Hudson Inc., 2000.

Pettis, Chuck. Secrets of Sacred Space. St. Paul, Minnesota: Llewellyn Publications, 1999.

Pollack, Rachel. The Body of the Goddess: Sacred Wisdom in Myth, Landscape and Culture. Rockport, Massachusetts: Element Books Limited, 1997.

Redmond, Layne. When the Drummers were Women: A Spiritual History of Rhythm. New York: Three Rivers Press, 1997.

Ronzani, Clare. Lecture, Psyche Soul and Spirit. Naropa University, Oakland, California, 2002.

Royal, Lyssa. "World Power Spots." Earth's Chakras. 1995. http://www.spiritweb.org/Spirit/world-power-spots.html (February 16, 2002).

Sahtouris, Elisabet. "Earthdance: Living Systems in Evolution." 1999. http://www.ratical.com/LifeWeb/Erthdnce/erthdnce.html (March 3, 2002).

Schultz, Mona Lisa. Awakening Intuition: Using Your Mind-Body Network for Insight and Healing. New York: Harmony Books, 1998.

Stewart, Sarah. Personal communication. September 1998; September 2001; June 2002.

Swan, James A. Sacred Places: How the Living earth Seeks our Friendship. Santa Fe, New Mexico: Bear and Company, Inc., 1990.

Swimme, Brian. Lecture, Creation Spirituality Intensive, Naropa University, Oakland, California; September 10, 2001.

---   The Hidden Heart of the Cosmos: Humanity and the New Story. Maryknoll, New York: Orbis Books, 1996.

Swimme, Brian and Thomas Berry. The Universe Story From the Primordial Flaring Forth to the Ecozoic Era: A Celebration of the Unfolding of the Cosmos. San Francisco: HarperCollins, 1994.

U.S. Forest Service. Palatki and Honanki Ruins. ND. http://aztec.asu.edu/aznha/palatki/paldoc.html. (February 7, 2002).

Vishnu," Microsoft Encarta Online Encyclopedia 2000; http://encarta.msn.com. 2000. (October 28, 2001).

"Vortex Energy." ND. http://www.sedonavortex.com/vortexenergy.htm. (November 27, 2001).

Vortexes of Earth Energy: Earth Magic–Turning into Our Mother at Rajuna's Refuge. http://www.angelfire.com/in/RajunasRefuge/vortexes.html, May 23, 2001; (October 2001).

Walker, Barbara G. The Woman's Encyclopedia of Myths and Secrets. San Francisco: HarperCollins, 1983.

---   The Woman's Dictionary of Symbols and Sacred Objects. San Francisco: HarperCollins, 1988

Printed in the United States
By Bookmasters